# TELL ME WHY

## ALSO BY ERIC WALTERS

# TELL ME WHY

## HOW YOUNG PEOPLE CAN CHANGE THE WORLD

### EDITED BY
# ERIC WALTERS

DOUBLEDAY
CANADA

Doubleday Canada and colophon are trademarks

Library and Archives Canada Cataloguing in Publication

Walters, Eric, 1957–
Tell me why : how young people can change the world /
Eric Walters.

ISBN 978-0-385-66720-3

1. Social justice—Juvenile literature.  2. Social action—
Juvenile literature.  3. Social problems—Juvenile literature.  4. Conduct of life—Juvenile literature.  I. Title.

HM671.W34 2009     j303.3'72     C2008-906945-5

Printed and bound in the USA

Published in Canada by Doubleday Canada,
a division of Random House of Canada Limited

Visit Random House of Canada Limited's website:
www.randomhouse.ca

10 9 8 7 6 5 4 3 2

This book is dedicated to the people who contributed to this book—young and not so young—who lead the way through their actions, words, and thoughts.

They are all heroes.

# INTRODUCTION

Sometimes you know where a book begins and sometimes you don't. I know where this one came from.

As a children's writer, teacher, social worker, and parent I have a great deal of contact with children and young adults. I have watched as they grow older and become aware of the larger world around them. Part of this awareness is learning about events that are often tragic—events that confuse and disturb them.

As an author, I travel across the country speaking to hundreds of thousands of young people. Many of my books have dealt with difficult subjects including genocide (*Shattered*), terrorism (*We All Fall Down*), street kids (*Sketches*), and children affected by war (*When Elephants Fight*). After these presentations, kids would often ask me questions about these situations, about human nature, about why people treat each other so badly, asking about good and evil, and what if anything they could possibly do to make an impact. I always tried my best to answer them. Sometimes, though, it felt more like I was just giving excuses than answers. These young people genuinely wanted to know the answers. And, quite frankly, so did I.

One night I woke up around three in the morning. I was thinking about some project or idea. I don't even remember what it was, but what I do remember that was in the middle of the night I had doubts. After sitting and thinking and worrying and wondering I sat down at my computer and wrote an e-mail to my friend Chandra— I feel so honoured to even say that—*my friend,* Chandra. I needed to talk to somebody. I needed advice. I needed his wisdom.

I told him about what I was working on, what I was doing, my worries and concerns about whether I'd bitten off more than I could chew. Satisfied, feeling a little better just putting down my thoughts, I sent the e-mail and got ready to go back to bed. Three minutes later I got a reply—it wasn't three in the morning in India where he lives and where he runs his orphanage.

His answer was simple. He told me that he had faith in the plan, and more importantly, in me and my ability to complete it. He told me he had no doubts and that neither should I. And because he said it, I knew it was right.

This is where this project started. I was blessed to have somebody like him to turn to—a person not only of compassion and dedication, but wisdom. I just wished that other people—especially children—had somebody like him to write to.

I started to wonder about how people would respond to a letter—a letter asking the questions kids were asking me. I worked with a group of seventy Grade 7 and 8 students at Pierre Elliott Trudeau Public School in Oshawa. They helped me to craft a letter that reflected the questions young people needed to ask. And while I made up Jo, the questions that Jo is asking are genuine and real.

I approached a diverse and eclectic group of individuals from the world of politics, entertainment, science, sports, and the arts. From astronaut, to opera singer, to cartoonist, to tight rope walker, to basketball player, to politician, this is a group that spans the range of human activities.

While they come from very different worlds they all share the same common trait. These are people who not only care, but have actively worked to make a difference. They are all genuine heroes.

Still trying to seek answers, I sought out the wisdom of some of my other heroes. I went back through time to find the words of wisdom of the greatest minds, the greatest humanitarians in history. Contained in this book are quotes from Socrates, Dr. Martin Luther King, Gandhi, Buddha, Mohammad, Jesus, Nelson Mandela, and Mother Teresa—quotes that speak directly to the questions posed by Jo.

The final part is not looking back in time, but toward the future. One of Jo's questions is, "What, if anything, do you think one kid can do to make a difference?" Profiled are five young people who are not only talking about making the world a better place, but *are* making the world the better place. These young people are the ultimate role models. I hope in their deeds other young people will be inspired not only to think, but do, that they will understand that greatest is contained within each of us—that to quote from the letter of one of the respondents, Dr. Lloyd Axworthy, "It is important to remember that within each Mother Teresa, within each Mahatma Gandhi, within the heroes among us who have given of themselves to make a difference in the world, there is a small boy or girl who began by asking these same very valuable questions."

Peace,
Eric Walters

PART 1

Hello,

My name is Jo. You don't know me, but I was wondering if you could help me. In school, over the past few months, we've been studying current events. Maybe I should have known better or been reading the papers, but I've been learning about terrible things that are happening in places I didn't even know existed. The more I read and hear, the more confused and upset I get.

It seems like there are tragedies everywhere. Floods, earthquakes, tornadoes, droughts, and famines—things my teacher calls natural disasters. Then there are accidents. It seems like every day there's a bus running off the road, or a ferry boat sinking, or a plane crashing. These are all bad things, terrible tragedies, but at least they aren't done on purpose.

What really bothers me the most, what really upsets me, is what people do to other people. Wars are being fought everywhere. Innocent people are being killed in battles over land or oil or money. Stranger still, wars are being fought because people have different ideas about who, or what, God is.

Just as bad are those cases where people die not because somebody did something, but because nobody did *anything*. I've learned that millions of people around the world die every year because they didn't have food or clean water or medicine.

There's no war where I live. We also have food and water. More than we could ever use. We have hospitals and medicines. Somehow, we have so much while so many people have so little.

I've talked to my friends and my teachers and my parents and my grandparents. I've asked them to explain to me how people can be so cruel or indifferent to each other. They try to explain, but they really don't seem to know either. One of my teachers said it was better to light a candle than to curse the darkness. I understand what she meant—it's better to try to do something, even something small, instead of just giving up and doing nothing. But, what does that actually mean in the real world?

I don't really know you, but from what I've read and heard, I know that you're a very smart person—and, even better, a smart person who tries to make a difference, who tries to help people. I was hoping that you could answer a few questions for me. Why do you think people treat each other the way that they do? Is there something that happened to you that made you want to help people? And finally, what, if anything, do you think one kid can do to make a difference? I know you're really busy, and you probably get bugged by people all the time, but if you could answer my letter I'd really appreciate it. I'd really like to know.

Sincerely,

Jo

P.S. Thanks for reading my letter and I'll understand if you don't write back.

# SUSAN AGLUKARK

Susan Aglukark was born on January 27, 1967, in Churchill, Manitoba. After high school she worked for the Department of Indian and Northern Affairs and began to perform as a singer in Inuit communities, where her acclaim and popularity grew quickly. Susan's first independent album, *Arctic Rose,* was released in 1992 and, in 1995, with her single "O Siem," she became the first Inuk performer to achieve a Top 40 hit in Canada, ultimately reaching number one.

Susan blends English and Inuktitut to tell the stories of her people through traditional and contemporary music. She has tackled difficult topics such as suicide and sexual abuse with sensitivity and has become a spokesperson for Aboriginal and Inuit youth and the challenges they face. Her gifts and passion have allowed her to become a motivational speaker for both youth and adults, providing political, cultural, and social awareness for all.

Susan has performed before dignitaries such as Queen Elizabeth II and Nelson Mandela and has toured the remote Aboriginal villages of the North. Among numerous honours, Susan became a member of the Order of Canada in September 2005, has been awarded three Juno

The smallest good deed is better than the grandest good intention.

*Unknown*

4

Awards, and received the first-ever Aboriginal Achievement Award in arts and entertainment.

Susan lives in Oakville, Ontario, with her husband and son and continues to touch lives through music, performance, and motivational speaking.

For more information: **www.susanaglukark.com**

Susan Aglukark

**Never doubt that a small group of thoughtful, committed citizens can change the world. Indeed, it is the only thing that ever has.**

*Margaret Mead*
*(American anthropologist, 1901–1978)*

Hello Jo,

I want to answer your letter with a story.

The Cherokee believe that the sun was a young woman who lived in the East and that the moon was her brother who lived in the West. Another story tells of the Redbird being the daughter of the sun. We all need to believe in something.

Maybe bad things happen because we lose the will to believe. The native Indians believed in a greater being they call the creator, that this greater being created the sun and the moon and the stars. But what's important isn't the connection between the people believing and what they believe in; instead, it's the simple act of believing, trusting so completely in something that it keeps you alive somewhere deep inside yourself, no matter what.

We don't ask for any of the bad things that happen to us, whether they be natural disasters or man-made disasters that have a big impact on innocent people. Whether they are bad people hurting us or us witnessing someone else being hurt, a lot of these things

## A mighty flame followeth a tiny spark.

**Dante Alighieri**
*(Italian poet, 1265–1321)*

happen because we aren't using the information given to us that would probably help to prevent them.

For example, we know better now why the earth is "hurting," and we know what we need to do to help it recover. Yet, most of us are not doing these things.

We know what hurts us and we know we can prevent that hurt, and we do try. Yet, every day we hear about more people being hurt. I think it's because many people have stopped believing, many have stopped truly wanting good things in life, many have forgotten that the simple act of self-respect and respecting others and everything around you is a powerful motivator to do good and to be good.

I was born and then raised in communities throughout the North. I was immersed in the history and stories of my culture, the native peoples of the North, aware of the strength necessary to survive. These are things that shaped my life.

I am also painfully aware of the problems within these communities—alcoholism, child

**By doing good we become good.**

*Jean-Jacques Rousseau (French philosopher, 1712–1778)*

abuse, displacement, and suicide—and how these have created despair, doubt, and low self-esteem. I have seen the pain. I have felt the pain. And while these obstacles are real, the greatest obstacles are all self-imposed. My message is about overcoming these obstacles, fostering self-respect and self-determination, and moving beyond those limitations.

> **Do not be overcome by evil, but overcome evil with good.**
>
> *St. Paul*

Like the native people—Indian, Metis, and Inuit—who simply chose to believe in something even though they never actually saw it, we need to trust again in the simple act of believing and allow that belief to keep awake in all of us, no matter what, the love for life, all of life.

I have faith in people, but even greater faith in young people's ability to change the world.

Susan

# LLOYD AXWORTHY

Dr. Lloyd Axworthy was born on December 21, 1939, in North Battleford, Saskatchewan, and raised in Winnipeg, Manitoba. He received a B.A. from the University of Winnipeg and a master's and Ph.D. from Princeton. He also was a student activist, putting into practice the lessons instilled in him by his mother, Gwen, to help those in need and speak for those without a voice.

Upon graduation, Lloyd entered politics, an area where he felt that a committed individual could make positive changes and affect the lives of others. He was a member of the Manitoba provincial assembly for six years and subsequently ran in the federal election. He was elected six times and sat in the House of Commons as a Liberal MP for twenty-one years before his retirement in 2000. He served in many Cabinet positions, including Minister of Foreign Affairs from 1996 to 2000. While serving in this capacity, he initiated international efforts to ban anti-personnel mines. His efforts culminated in the Ottawa Treaty, which called for the prohibition of the use, stockpiling, production, or transfer of anti-personnel mines. Ultimately, 157 countries signed this accord and Lloyd was nominated for the Nobel Peace Prize for his leadership.

**Vision without action is a daydream. Action without vision is a nightmare.**

*Japanese proverb*

> **You must be the change you wish to see in the world.**
>
> *Mahatma Gandhi*
> *(Indian politician, activist, and visionary, 1869–1948)*

After retiring from politics, Lloyd was involved in Human Rights Watch and was the director of the Liu Centre for the Study of Global Issues. He has received numerous honours and awards, including the Madison medal from Princeton, the CARE International Humanitarian Award, the Thakore Award honouring Mahatma Gandhi's peace work, the North-South Institutes Peace Award, and the Order of Canada. He has written many reports and books, including *Navigating a New World: Canada's Global Future*.

Lloyd resides in Winnipeg with his wife, Denise, but is a global citizen who uses his voice, vision, and diplomacy to advance human security and peace. He is President and Vice-Chancellor of the University of Winnipeg.

Lloyd
Axworthy

Dear Jo,

It seems as though there has always been conflict, always been suffering, and always been a division between those who have more than they need and those who do not have nearly enough. I cannot tell you why that is any more than I can tell you why some people hurt others, whether willingly or through indifference. What I can tell you is that within every person who cares to ask why, there is the potential to make a difference in the world.

I am reminded of an observation made by Susan Sontag in her book *Regarding the Pain of Others,* written just before her death. She wrote of how we have increasingly become a "society of spectacle," witnessing through the transmission of photography, television, or computer screen the horrors being suffered in distant parts of the world while enjoying the comfort and security of our privileged existence. As she says, "Being a spectator of calamities taking place in another country is a quintessential modern experience . . . 'If it bleeds it leads' runs the venerable guideline of tabloids and twenty-four-hour headline news shows—to which the

> **To overcome evil with good is good, to resist evil with evil is evil.**
>
> **Muhammad**
> *(Prophet and founder of Islam, 570–632)*

response is compassion, or indignation, or tit-illation, or approval, as each misery heaves into view."

How many "calamities," whether natural or man-made, have become part of our living experience, been absorbed into our mental membrane, searing our moral essence? Or have they already faded into the archives of the ongoing inhumanity of man? How often have we quickly changed the channel when some attempt was made to ask questions about why such calamities continue to hap-pen and why our response is so predictably ad hoc and short term?

Every kindness makes a difference, whether it is fundraising for a worthy cause, petitioning and lobbying for change, or simply sharing a smile with someone who doesn't have one of their own. A difference can be achieved through grand gestures, but also through everyday acts of kindness. Once you accept this, the world's problems cease to seem quite so insurmountable.

To give you an example, right here in Canada, a number of concerned citizens, groups, and

I do not feel obligated to believe that the same God who has endowed us with sense, reason, and intellect has intended us to forgo their use.

**Galileo**
*(Italian artist, inventor, and genius, 1564–1642)*

officials worked together to bring about an international ban on the use of land mines. It was a huge effort on the part of many people. The one thing that all of those people had in common was the belief that they could make a difference, that their efforts and their persistence could help others and could lead to substantive changes for the better.

I understand that it can become very disheartening at times to hear of the daily tragedies that many people endure. And at times it can seem overwhelming and pointless to even try to work toward change. When the world's problems seem too large to tackle, it is important to remember that within each Mother Teresa, within each Mahatma Gandhi, within the heroes among us who have given of themselves to help make a difference in the world, there was once a small boy or girl who began by asking the same very valuable questions that you are asking. The greatest wrongs in the world are enabled not by malice alone, but also by indifference. That is why it is so very important to never stop asking why.

Lloyd

**In charity there is no excess.**

*Sir Francis Bacon*
*(British scientist and philosopher, 1561–1626)*

# MAUDE BARLOW

Maude Barlow is the National Chairperson of the Council of Canadians and Senior Advisor on Water to the President of the UN General Assembly. She serves on the boards of the International Forum of Globalization and Food and Water Watch, as well as being a Councillor with the Hamburg-based World Future Council and the bestselling author or co-author of fifteen books. She has received many awards, including honorary doctorates from six Canadian universities as well as the 2005 Right Livelihood Award, given by the Swedish Parliament for her international work on the right to water and widely referred to as the "Alternative Nobel."

To contact the Council of Canadians, go to www.canadians.org

> "Few will have the greatness to bend history itself, but each of us can work to change a small portion of events, and in the total of all those acts will be written the history of this generation."
>
> *Robert F. Kennedy*
> *(American politician,*
> *1925–1968)*

Maude Barlow

Dear Jo,

The answer to your questions is of course very complicated. For some people, there has been no moral grounding, no one to set an example, a childhood without love or guidance. Some are anxious or even desperate to succeed in a materialistic, competitive and hierarchical society. Some are affected by fundamentalism that exists on the edges of most religions, even to the point of embracing violence. Many are victims of a world that has become deeply divided by class and income disparities; denied education, basic health care, decent food, even clean water.

> "Kindness is the golden chain by which society is bound together."
>
> *Johann Wolfgang von Goethe*
> *(German author, 1749–1832)*

What is crucial to understand is that humanity will never eradicate violence or the collective rage of whole groups until we address social inequality and economic injustice. This will require those of us living in the global North to change our priorities and create more just international institutions and more sustainable trade and economic policies. Our present system creates and cements entrenched social differences. While a minority gets wealthier, the majority sinks deeper into poverty. Changing this reality has to be our collective priority.

I cannot say that it was any one event that made a difference to me, rather a series of events filtered through the lens of my childhood. I was fortunate enough to have wonderful parents who taught me that if one is lucky enough to be born in this country, one owes something back to the greater society. My father, William McGrath, led the fight in Canada against capital punishment so I came to my activism early.

What I can say is that I maintain a great sense of hope, which is crucial to my kind of work. I believe that hope is a moral imperative. It is easy to get overwhelmed when one is confronted by terrible poverty, injustice or environmental devastation. The hard part is staying focussed, not on the outcome alone (for no one person ever determines that), but on what you can do in your own small way. The terrible statistics on ecological damage, for example, do not take into account the effect that millions of committed people around the world are making to save the environment. Attitudes

"The life I touch for good or ill will touch another life, and that in turn another, until who knows where the trembling stops or in what far place my touch will be felt."

*Frederick Buechner*
*(American author, 1926–)*

*can* change. Activism and commitment *do* make a difference.

What can one young person do to make a difference?

Oh, so much that I don't know where to begin. First you must determine that you want to make a difference and set out to learn as much as you can about the world around you and your opportunities for activism. It is crucial to seek out like-minded people of your own age but also of other ages who can work with you and guide you. Decide to live your principles, remembering that every racist, homophobic or cruel statement or act is a drop of poison in an already polluted world. Decide not to add any poison in your world.

As well, it is very important to examine critically the ideologies, structures and systems in our society that deliberately create winners and losers and that thrive on inequality and injustice. Unless we challenge the systems that keep people poor or exploit the natural environment, we will only be delivering charity, not essential change. Charity

"You are the people who are shaping a better world. One of the secrets of inner peace is the practice of compassion."

*Dalai Lama*
*(Tibetan spiritual leader, 1935–)*

does not challenge the status quo and often is used to assuage the guilt of the powerful whose day-to-day acts perpetuate the very problems their acts of charity seek to address.

Most of all, have a wonderful time being an activist. It is the best life you can choose. You will meet the best people and go to sleep at night with a clear conscience, which my dad always said, makes the best pillow.

Sincerely,
Maude Barlow

"We cannot live for ourselves alone. Our lives are connected by a thousand invisible threads, and along these sympathetic fibers, our actions run as causes and return to us as results."

*Herman Melville*
*(American author*
*1819–1891)*

# BELLADONNA

Belladonna eats words and spits hot fire, conceiving works across various media, including hip hop, spoken word, theatre, comedy, dance, and the indefinable. Originally from Grenada in the West Indies, Belladonna endeavours to infuse all of her work with a sense of joy and purpose, aligning herself with such organizations as Face in the Crowd Collective (ARCfest), Project Humanity (Save Darfur), Athletes for Africa (Guluwalk), Oxfam (Music4Change), YWCA (Week Without Violence), as well as Toronto East for Peace, Artists Against War, and the National Action Committee on the Status of Women. Belladonna is currently the general manager for Native Earth Performing Arts, lead vocalist with Belladonna & the Awakening, and a member of Obsidian Theatre Company's inaugural playwriting unit. She believes that change is possible.

For more information:
**www.freethechildren.com**
**www.guluwalk.com**
**www.athletesforafrica.com**

**If a free society cannot help the many who are poor, it cannot save the few who are rich.**

*John F. Kennedy*
*(American president,*
*1917–1963)*

Jo,

Thanks for writing to me about your questions. I am not surprised you find this confusing—so do I.

I was once on a subway platform in Toronto, having an argument with my boyfriend. At first it was only verbal, but all of a sudden he stopped yelling and punched me in the stomach. I doubled over in surprise and pain. As I straightened up, wind rushed past me and my ears filled with the screeching of metal as the train pulled in. He punched me again. The train's doors opened and people flooded out . . . and walked right past what they had just seen. I thought, *This person who I love is not doing this. These people, who I believe are good people, are not letting him. This time that I live in will not allow it.* I saw them make way for him to pass through, everybody doing their best not to look at me. In seconds, I was left alone on the platform, confused.

My life is full of times when I wish someone had spoken up. I wish someone had said, "I won't let that happen." My life is full of

Whether you think you can, or that you can't, you are usually right.

*Henry Ford*
*(American inventor and innovator, 1863–1947)*

moments when I was surprised to find myself alone.

Some of the things going on in the world right now remind me of that experience. You're right that we have so much, and share so little in the world's suffering. In a way, we are like the people on that train pulling into the station, watching something happen and deciding if we will allow it.

Now, when I think about that day, I think I know why no one stopped. It is the same reason they made way for my boyfriend to get past: they were afraid. I believe that they wished it hadn't happened, and so they tried to pretend it hadn't. In the same way that the experience affected me, I know it affected them, too. They went home knowing they had done nothing.

Fear is a powerful thing. It does something to people. They are afraid to know what is happening, especially if they think they are not strong enough to help. They are afraid that knowing will make them feel powerless; they don't realize that not wanting to know empowers oppression. They are afraid that

**Waste no more time arguing about what a good man should be. Be one.**

**Marcus Aurelius**
*(Roman emperor, 121–180)*

knowing will make them give up; they don't realize that doing nothing is giving up in advance. They are afraid that knowing will hurt them; they don't realize that by refusing to know they hurt themselves and others. They are afraid that knowing will make them sad; they don't realize that joyfulness is a powerful force for change. They are afraid that knowing will make them hate; they don't realize that caring for others makes us love, makes us human. Every time I think of this, I see them seeing me, and I know that silence hurts more than a punch in the gut.

Fear can make people do terrible things to each other. My boyfriend thought I would leave him if he didn't make me stay, and he was afraid of being alone and unloved. Other people fear being small and unimportant, or fear that they will be hurt if they don't hurt someone else first.

I know you feel like you're just a kid, but you are so powerful. There is so much you can do. I want to thank you for asking questions and I want you to keep asking them. Ask why something is happening, and why we are letting it happen. Don't be afraid to step onto

> We must learn to live together as brothers or perish together as fools.
>
> *Martin Luther King, Jr.*
> *(American activist, visionary, and minister, 1929–1968)*

the platform and say, "This has to stop." If you are brave enough to say it first, you make it possible for others to say it, too. If you see others saying it first, stand with them so that they will know they are not alone. Know that having courage does not mean that you are not afraid. It means that you are willing to overcome your fear and do what is right.

If you had seen me take a punch on that platform, I believe that you would have asked, "Why are we letting this happen?" You don't have to take the punch for me, you just have to say that it is wrong. Thank you for not standing by.

Love,
Belladonna

The humblest individual exerts some influence, either for good or evil, upon others.

**Henry Ward Beecher**
*(American clergyman and slavery abolitionist, 1813–1887)*

Belladonna

# ADRIAN BRADBURY

It's kind of fun to do the impossible.

**Walt Disney**
*(American animator and innovator, 1901–1966)*

Adrian Bradbury was born on April 5, 1970, in Oshawa, Ontario. He graduated from the University of Ottawa, where he played on the school's basketball team. Adrian combined his love of sports and his awareness of global issues to found Athletes for Africa, a charitable organization that uses the power and profile of sport to educate individuals and engage countries in Africa's fight against poverty, famine, and disease.

Adrian became aware of the plight of children in the all-but-forgotten twenty-year civil war in Uganda. With co-founder Kieran Hayward, he created Guluwalk. Together, they engaged in a thirty-one-day "night commute" to bring to light the tragedy of the forty thousand children living in rural northern Uganda who were forced to flee nightly to escape death or abduction into the life of a child soldier or sex slave.

In 2006, eighty-two cities in fifteen countries participated simultaneously in GuluWalk Day, raising more than $500,000 for rehabilitation, training, and health support programs for the children of northern Uganda.

Adrian lives in Toronto with his wife, Kim, and their two sons, Isaac and Owen. He travels extensively, meeting with local people, community leaders, politicians, and members of the media in his continued efforts to champion the cause of the children in Uganda.

For more information: **www.guluwalk.com**

Adrian Bradbury

**Where there is no struggle, there is no strength.**

*Oprah Winfrey*
*(American broadcaster*
*and humanitarian, 1954–)*

Dear Jo,

In our country, when a child goes missing we react with horror and the entire nation rushes to help. There are pictures in the newspapers and appeals for help on the television, alerts are sent out, police and volunteers scour the area for clues, and the whole country shares in the family's grief, hoping to help find the missing child somehow and reunite the family. You've probably seen these pictures and felt this sadness. That's the way it should be.

> Courage, my friends; 'tis not too late to build a better world.
>
> *Tommy Douglas*
> *(Canadian politician and clergyman, 1904–1986)*

Unfortunately, that isn't the case in some places.

In Uganda, tens of thousands of children are killed or abducted, yet we sit by idly. In the past twenty years, more than forty thousand children have suffered that fate in Uganda, but the situation is largely unknown or it is ignored.

In Gulu, Uganda, a little boy was born on April 5, 1970. He grew up witnessing terror, fearing for his life and the lives of his family, forced to flee every night, leaving his home behind, seeking shelter. He now lives in an internally displaced persons camp where more than a thousand people are dying every week from violence, hunger, and preventable diseases.

April 5, 1970, is also my birthday. The only difference between me and that boy is that, on that spring day in 1970, he was born into a war zone and I was born into the lap of luxury in Toronto, Canada. Why do I have so much, why do *we all* have so much, more than we could ever need, while others have so little?

**Softness can conquer hardness.**

*Principle of Tai-Chi*

Maybe a turning point for me in needing to do more was the birth of my first child. I knew how much love I felt, but also realized that parents around the world felt that same joy, that same love for their children. We are all people, not statistics. I stopped seeing the numbers and started seeing the faces. These are not numbers we're talking about; they're people just like you and me, like your family and my family.

I work to try to help the children of Gulu, Uganda. I get incredible joy from helping to change the situation there, from bettering their lives. I try to remember the words of Albert Einstein: "Setting an example is not the main means of influencing another, it is the only means." You can't put it more perfectly than that.

Human rights should mean more than a piece of paper that says we care. Human rights only matters when we stop talking about it and actually do something. That's how we can make a difference.

> Non-cooperation with evil is as much a duty as is cooperation with good.
>
> *Mahatma Gandhi*
> *(Indian politician, activist, and visionary, 1869–1948)*

You are only one person, but everything starts with one person. Keep asking why. Keep telling your story. Take action and you'll be the difference-maker you want to be—and that, too, will change you for the better, more than you could ever imagine.

In Peace,
Adrian

# GERALD CAPLAN

Gerald Caplan has a master's in Canadian history from the University of Toronto and a Ph.D. in African history from the School of Oriental and African Studies at the University of London. He has been a lifelong social and political activist with close ties to the New Democratic Party of Canada and a commitment to African development.

A former associate professor in the Department of History and Philosophy of Education at the Ontario Institute for Studies in Education (OISE)/University of Toronto, he is the author of numerous books, articles, reports, and book reviews. Among his recent major publications were essays on genocide and Africa in *Walrus* magazine and a comprehensive report called *Rwanda: The Preventable Genocide* prepared for the International Panel of Eminent Personalities established by the Organization of African Unity to investigate the genocide.

In recent years, Gerald has been a consultant for the United Nations' Special Coordinator for Africa, the Economic Commission for Africa in which he documents the case he makes in his letter to Jo about who is responsible for Africa's many problems today, the United Nations

**Human history becomes more and more a race between education and catastrophe.**

*H.G. Wells*
*(English novelist and futurist, 1866–1946)*

Development Program, UNICEF, the World Health Organization, and the African Union.

His major preoccupations are African development, AIDS, and genocide. He was the volunteer chair of the International Advisory Board for the African AIDS Initiative of the University of Toronto as well as senior adviser to Stephen Lewis when he was UN Special Envoy for AIDS in Africa. He has developed a course on the Rwandan genocide, which he teaches at the University for Peace, and he advises solidarity groups on genocide prevention and the crises in Darfur and northern Uganda.

He continues to provide public commentary on African development issues and genocide prevention and speaks internationally on these issues. His latest book is *The Betrayal of Africa*.

> **Be great in act, as you have been in thought.**
>
> **William Shakespeare**
> *(English playwright, 1564–1616)*

Gerald Caplan

Dear Jo,

I've been studying, teaching about, and working in poor countries my entire life, especially those in Africa. I'm also deeply concerned about the great differences that exist in the lives led by people in rich countries and poor countries. As everybody knows, Africa faces enormous problems. It has suffered from terrible history, terrible leaders, terrible policies, and terrible wars. Often, people in our rich world blame Africans themselves for their difficult fate and believe that what Africans need most is for rich, white Western folk to save them from themselves.

Well, it's true that people are never just innocent victims, and that Africans can't escape some responsibility for their plight. But not all Africans. I blame most of Africa's leaders for being motivated by greed and power and for being uninterested in the welfare of their people. But I equally accuse the leaders of the rich world—including Canada—of imposing on Africa both leaders and policies that have caused enormous suffering for hundreds of millions of Africans. I assure

> We have too many high-sounding words, and too few actions that correspond with them.
>
> **Abigail Adams**
> *(American writer and wife of President John Adams, 1744–1818)*

you that there is a great deal of evidence for this shocking accusation.

That's why people like me continue to fight so that Africans can have a better, more secure life. It's not because I'm a nice guy, or a great humanitarian, or that I'm better or smarter than Africans. It's because I've learned that we've become the most prosperous society in the history of the world partly because we've exploited African societies so shamelessly. We owe it to Africa to make up for what we've done to it and what we've stolen from it.

It's a very hard, uphill battle, and I hope you decide to join it. But don't think you'll be alone. There are many of us in the rich countries who see things this way. What's even better, there are tens of millions of Africans who are dedicating their lives to making their continent a better place for all to live and thrive.

It's true that people often do terrible things to each other. I'm afraid this has been a reality of our species ever since we evolved into human beings long, long ago. On the

How wonderful it is that we can start doing good deeds at this very moment.

**Anne Frank**
*(German writer and Holocaust victim, 1929–1945)*

one hand, unlike animals, we humans are capable of showing love, respect, and compassion for each other. On the other hand, it's sad to say, we're also capable of treating each other in sick and disgusting ways. I'd say that the evidence is pretty strong that there is, in every one of us, the capacity to behave in either way. It really depends on the circumstances each of us grows up in, which mostly has little to do with anything we can control. Therefore, the job of humankind must be to work as hard as possible to create a world where most people grow up in conditions that bring out our better side instead of our darker one.

Maybe we in the West can repay our enormous debt. Working together with our African colleagues, I believe we can really make a difference. But we really need your help, Jo. Together, we can make a difference in their lives, and in doing so, make a difference in our own lives.

Gerald

We have a Call to do good, as often as we have the Power and Occasion.

**William Penn**
*(English religious leader, 1644–1718)*

# DR. CHANDRA

Dr. Chandra Sekhar Sankurathri was born on November 20, 1943, in Andhra Pradesh, India. He received a B.Sc. and M.Sc. in zoology from Andhra University, and M.Sc. in biology from Memorial University, and his Ph.D. in zoology from the University of Alberta. He and his wife moved to Ottawa to work for Environment Canada and then Health and Welfare Canada, and to raise a family.

On June 23, 1985, his wife, Manjari, and children, Srikiran, age 6, and Saranda, age 3, were killed when their Air India flight was bombed by terrorists. This devastating loss left Dr. Chandra searching for a way to bring meaning back into his life.

He chose to overcome his personal grief by helping others. He returned to India to dedicate his life to serving the poor in rural areas near Kakinada, East Godavari District, the area where he was born. In 1989, he founded the Manjari Sankurathri Memorial Foundation. He established a primary school in Andhra Pradesh, dedicated to providing free quality education to local children. In 1993, the Srikiran Institute of Ophthalmology was established with sixty beds as well as outpatient outreach programs.

Distance does not decide who is your brother and who is not.

**Bono**
*(Irish musician and social activist, 1960–)*

34

It provides extensive eye care to the rural poor through eye camps, patient care, surgical interventions, and childhood blindness control. The foundation continues to expand its focus to provide basic necessities such as food, drinking water, medical aid, medication, and clothing in times of emergency.

Dr. Chandra has received many honours and awards, including the Mother Teresa Excellence Award and the Sankalp Tara Award for rendering service to the needy, as well as awards from the Rotary Club, the Lions Club, and the Telugu Cultural Society.

For more information: **www.msmf.ca**

**Words without actions are the assassins of idealism.**

**Herbert Hoover**
*(American president, 1874–1964)*

Dr. Chandra

Dear Jo,

Greetings from Sankurathri Foundation, Kakinada, Andhra Pradesh, India.

Just like you, I have been asking these same questions for a long time, but I never got direct answers from anyone. I will try to put down my thoughts about your questions.

> The actions of men are the best interpreters of their thoughts.
>
> *John Locke*
> *(English philosopher, 1632–1704)*

I have been affected by terrorism. My wife and two children were killed while travelling from Canada to India. Their plane exploded from a terrorist bomb while crossing the Atlantic Ocean and all 329 people aboard were killed. I had seen them off at the airport in Montreal only a few hours earlier; then they vanished into thin air. Why did this happen? What did they do to deserve this kind of death? Why has God punished me like this? Who has deprived me of my beloved family? Why did they do this act? Who has the right to kill 329 innocent people? Why and how did the culprits get away with this mass murder? How can we prevent such terrible acts in the future? The questions go on and on . . . but there are no answers.

With this act of terrorism my life was devastated; I didn't know what to do and from whom to seek help. I was so lost and do not know how I survived the next three years. I could not accept the fact that my family would never return to me.

After struggling for three years and feeling sorry for my loss, I thought my life should have purpose. I was only forty-two years old and needed to make a difference in others' lives. I thought I should stop feeling sorry for myself and divert my love and affection for my family toward people in despair. Because of this change in attitude I am now able to help many people and make a difference in their lives.

Your teacher said the right thing. If there is darkness, light one candle to dispel it. If a thousand people light a thousand candles, the darkness will disappear. Nothing could be better than that. There is an old saying that every drop will eventually fill the bucket.

That is exactly what we are doing here. We have been lighting several thousand lights in the lives of the blind by performing cataract

> **The best preparation for good work tomorrow is to do good work today.**
>
> *Elbert Hubbard*
> *(American author, 1956–1915)*

surgeries and restoring vision. So far, we have restored eyesight to more than 140,000 people who would have remained blind if we had not intervened. Similarly, we have prevented blindness in several thousands by intervening at the right time.

In the last fifteen years, we have provided value-added quality education to more than a thousand children from poor rural families. As a result, we have already noticed changes in their attitude, behaviour, and performance. These are very positive changes that will benefit society in the long run.

These results make me happy because I am proving useful to many people. This gives me immense satisfaction and I feel I am doing good with my life. Because of my involvement in enhancing others' quality of life, I do not think about my personal loss anymore, and I live in peace. Now I have a mission, one that has no end in sight because there are always people less fortunate than we are. My mission will continue for as long as there is human suffering and misery due to blindness and illiteracy.

> The best way to find yourself is to lose yourself in the service of others.
>
> *Mahatma Gandhi*
> *(Indian politician, activist, and visionary, 1869–1948)*

I would not wish what I went through after the loss of my family on even my enemy. Do I have any enemies? No. I do not hate anyone, not even the people who placed bombs on that plane and killed my family. On the contrary, I feel sorry for them and pray to God that they will live in peace. That will happen only if they feel remorse for their terrible actions; otherwise, they will be hounded by their consciences.

I am touching several thousands of people's lives through my work. Anyone can do this, but many are not aware of others' need for help. You can increase awareness in society through charitable activities. We should all realize how lucky we are to be where we are and have what we have when compared to millions of people in other parts of the world. Even in our own area, not everyone is well off. We can help them, too.

Despite our diversity, there could be a common element of tolerance, understanding, and compassion toward others. If we could all achieve this quality, the world would be a better place to live. Because it is not possible to achieve an ideal situation, we are faced

> Justice consists not in being neutral between right and wrong, but in finding out the right and upholding it, wherever found, against the wrong.
>
> **Theodore Roosevelt**
> *(American president, 1858–1919)*

with all of these turmoils, wars, violence, terrorism, and social unrest. It may sound like
gloom and doom, but there is always hope to
make things better.

With love, compassion, and care, we can
communicate with and transform most
individuals. Love and affection are great
tools that give the best results, because they
always bounce back what we give. There is
no better method than to reform people and
integrate them into the mainstream of society. This is possible only when there is real
feeling toward these people, regardless of
race, religion, caste, class, age, sex, and other
socio-economic factors. Treat every human
being as one of us and try to relate to them.
There are great personalities in history who
have done this before and shown that it is
possible. Wherever there is human suffering
and frustration, there is the possibility of
unrest that will lead to violence. It is up to
us to create positive conditions and make
this world a better place to live.

What can a single individual do to bring
about change? Well, this single individual is
very important, and that person could be a

**Good thoughts are no better than good dreams, unless they be executed.**

*Ralph Waldo Emerson*
*(American poet and philosopher, 1803–1882)*

charismatic leader who can influence several millions of people and effect a change in them. We need many such individuals to make this a better place to live. To fill the ocean, we need many droplets of water; similarly, to bring about a big change in people's attitudes, we need many leaders who value human dignity, hate suffering, and thereby influence the people around them. Who knows—you could be one of those blossoming leaders!

What I do here came out of personal tragedy. Because of my loss I devote myself full-time to making a difference in society. But we do not all need to work full-time toward this goal. People have different priorities and they should fulfill their Dharma (duty) first. They can help by supporting the existing efforts of other individuals who reach out to the have-nots. By working together, we can achieve goals that would be unattainable by an individual. The secret is to work as a team for the best results.

I do not know where you live, but it doesn't matter. Any person with feelings and values would wonder about the events happening

> **We are all manufacturers. Making good, making trouble, or making excuses.**
>
> *H.V. Adolt*
> *(Author)*

in the world. Your questions show that you are a caring person who shares the grief and sorrow of others. I hope to see many more people like you in this world. If more people, especially children, ask these questions, we can create a better world.

With love,
Chandra

> Our scientific power has outrun our spiritual power. We have guided missiles and misguided men.
>
> *Martin Luther King, Jr.*
> *(American activist, visionary, and minister, 1929–1968)*

# JAY COCHRANE

Jay Cochrane was born on May 1, 1944, in Saint John, New Brunswick, and raised in Sudbury and North Bay, Ontario. At age 14, he ran away from home, joined the Royal Hanneford Circus, and was taken under the tutelage of famed aerialist Princess Tajana. Jay says, "Whatever I became, I owe it all to her." He quickly moved from cleaning animals to become an aerialist himself.

Already established as one of the finest aerialists alive, Jay's life was almost ended when a poorly constructed tower collapsed during his act and he plummeted thirty metres to a concrete floor. It was considered miraculous that he lived, and doctors believed he would never walk again. In a testament to his strength, perseverance, and determination, he not only started walking again, but resumed walking the high wire within four years.

Jay holds numerous world records, including longest time on a wire (21 days), farthest distance on a wire (2.5 miles), and the longest and highest combined skywalk (2098 feet long, 1340 feet high). This last record, a walk across the Qutang Gorge over the Yangtze River in China, was witnessed by 200,000 people, as

**Heaven is not reached at a single bound.**

*Unknown*

well as a television audience of more than 200 million, and is considered one of the greatest wire walks in history. It cemented Jay's place as the most accomplished aerialist of all time.

Jay now resides in Ocala, Florida. He continues his death-defying feats and uses his high wire as a platform to inspire, speak to the strength of the human spirit, and raise awareness of and funds for children's charities.

For more information: **www.jaycochrane.com**

MARK PHILLIPS

Jay Cochrane

**Our deepest fear is not that we are inadequate. Our deepest fear is that we are powerful beyond measure.**

*Marianne Williamson,*
*from* **A Return to Love: Reflections on the Principles of "A Course in Miracles"**
*(American writer and lecturer, 1952–)*

Dear Jo,

Many things in my life have led me to want to do things for others. When I first started out in the circus, we used to visit children in hospitals, in burn units, those sorts of wards. I was always amazed at the kids I met, at their courage. They seldom complained about their situation. They faced their problems head on and maintained marvellous, positive attitudes. It started me thinking that most of us were probably better people when we were kids and that we tend to lose our best qualities as we grow up: our innocence, our generosity, our positive thinking.

Then, in 1995, I was invited to go to China to walk over the famous Yangtze River on a sky wire about half a kilometre high, the greatest high wire in history, the world record. I was pretty excited about it, and a little nervous, thinking a great deal about myself and this monumental thing I was going to do, when suddenly something much more marvellous than any of that happened. Out of the hills, it seemed, a whole school of children appeared and began to sing a Chinese love song. It was very moving.

**It is astonishing how short a time it takes for very wonderful things to happen.**

*Frances Burnett*
*(American author,*
*1817–1862)*

I visited their homes and their facilities, and they had nothing, virtually nothing, especially compared to us. But they were beautiful, and what they were doing was magical. It really made me want to help others, especially disadvantaged children. I'd been doing that to a degree for a long time but, after that experience, I dedicated my life to it. Everywhere I go now, I raise money for children, for those who are sick and dying or who have little. It isn't a burden or a chore. It is an honour. I am trying to raise as many millions of dollars as I can.

I've often performed in the East, in China, and I've grown to love that culture. I like the way many of the common folks there treat one another. They have more time for each other than we do in the West. Here, it seems like we are always watching the latest soap opera, political scandal, or celebrity moment on TV, or playing the latest video game, instead of talking, trying to understand each other, and concerning ourselves with what really matters. We all do it. I know I do sometimes . . . I'll bet you do too. We need to do more soul-searching: turn off the TV, limit all of those superficial and often self-gratifying

> **In every community, there is work to be done. In every nation, there are wounds to heal. In every heart, there is the power to do it.**
>
> *Marianne Williamson*
> *(American writer and lecturer, 1952–)*

concerns. We need to think about others in a truly humane way. We need to get out and really interact with each other. And we need to treat others the way we would like to be treated. I have a saying: "Take ME and turn the first letter upside down . . . so it reads WE." We need to try to understand one another; we need to turn the ME into WE. If countries really understood others, could really feel for others, the world's problems would melt away.

I learned this not by being a big wire-walking star, but by experiencing things like those poor children singing on a hillside in China. They were rich in spirit, in innocence, and in kindness. We all need to be more like children: innocent, honest, and, for the most part, kind.

You asked what you can do. You can't change the world overnight, but you can make a difference. This may sound kind of corny, but oftentimes it's the little things in life that matter. Try to be good to the people in your life. Go up to another kid in your school, maybe someone you've never spoken to or someone others don't seem to like, and talk

**The only way to compel men to speak good of us is to do it.**

*Voltaire*
*(French dramatist and philosopher, 1694–1778)*

to that person. Don't look around at others as you talk; look right into that kid's eyes and ask how he or she is doing that day, compliment him or her . . . and really mean it. If everyone did that, or at least that sort of thing, we wouldn't have the problems we do: we'd have peace everywhere. You might say, "Mr. Cochrane, that's kind of silly. Would that really make a difference? Isn't that naive?" But that's precisely the problem. We think we need to be big, important people who will change the world overnight, instead of looking into each others' eyes and reaching out, being true friends to those around us.

We take nothing to our graves. We will be remembered for the way we have touched others, period. I've finally gotten that into my head. I no longer perform for records, for money, or for attention. I do it for the children of the world who don't have what they should have. I do it to touch others, to promote understanding, and to reach out to others. And I do it for young people, because they are our future.

**It is easy to be brave from a safe distance.**

***Aesop***
*(Turkish or Egyptian storyteller and philosopher, 620 BC–560 BC)*

We all need to be rich, but rich in kindness and understanding. Be that way yourself and see if you can spread it around. That's what I'm trying to do.

Jay Cochrane, "The Prince of the Air"

Believe, when you are most unhappy, there is something for you to do in the world. So long as you can sweeten another's pain, life is not in vain.

**Helen Keller**
(American author and activist, 1880–1968)

# LT.-GEN. ROMÉO DALLAIRE

When good people in any country cease their vigilance and struggle, then evil men prevail.

*Pearl S. Buck*
*(American writer,*
*1892–1973)*

Roméo Dallaire was born on June 25, 1946, in Denekamp, The Netherlands, while his father, a staff sergeant in the Canadian Forces, was stationed in that country. His family returned to Canada when he was six months old, and he was raised in Montreal. Roméo followed his family's military tradition, enlisting in the Canadian Army in 1964. He graduated from the Royal Military College in 1969 with a B.Sc. and was commissioned into the Royal Regiment of Canadian Artillery. A career soldier, he rose through the ranks and in July 1989 was promoted to brigadier general. From 1990 to 1993 he was the Commander of Collège Militaire Royal de Saint-Jean. In 1993, he received a commission as Force Commander of the United Nations Assistant Mission for Rwanda.

At that time, Rwanda was emerging from a long, deadly civil war, and Roméo's mission was to implement the terms of a peace accord between the warring factions. Once on the ground in Rwanda, he quickly realized that a great tragedy was being readied. His observations, reports, and requests for help went unheard. Rather than being given the mandate, men, and materials necessary to intervene, he became witness to a genocide in which more than 800,000 people were slaughtered. Unable to stop it, his valiant intervention saved the lives of tens of thousands of innocent people.

Roméo was given a medical release from the military in 2000 that led to a diagnosis of post-traumatic stress disorder. He left the military with the rank of lieutenant general, and was subsequently appointed to the Canadian Senate. He has become a human rights champion, travelling the world and speaking for those unable to speak for themselves. Roméo Dallaire: husband, father, soldier, senator, author, human rights activist, humanitarian, hero.

> # My country is the world, and my religion is to do good.
>
> **Thomas Paine**
> *(American author and revolutionary, 1737–1809)*

Roméo Dallaire

Dear Jo,

It is not often that I get a letter from someone your age that contains such big questions, and so I would like to thank you for writing. To answer one of your last questions first, the very fact that you are thinking about these things and asking questions encourages me to think that our youth will learn from our mistakes and shape a brighter future.

You've asked why I think people treat each other the way they do. I've often asked myself the same thing. As you probably know, I was the general in command of the United Nations mission for Rwanda in 1994, when neighbours rose up against neighbours, leaving more than 800,000 innocent men, women, and children dead in only a hundred days. During this time, the rest of the world sat back and watched, unmoved—or simply changed the channel. People died horribly and unnecessarily because, as you said, nobody did anything.

In writing about Rwanda, and in speaking about it, I have often asked, "Are all humans

**Love conquers all.**

*Horace*
*(Italian writer, 65 BC–8 BC)*

human, or are some more human than others?" One vision from Rwanda that I will never forget is that of a little boy, about three years old, wandering alone in the middle of the road. As I picked him up, I was struck by the fact that I could have been staring into the eyes of my own three-year-old son. We are all human, and not one of us is worth more or less than another. Just as we have a capacity for cruelty, we also have a capacity for compassion and humanity. The difference is in the choices each of us makes.

I know that, as a kid, it sometimes feels like you can't possibly do anything that will make a difference. (Believe me, adults sometimes feel the same way.) Remember, though, that Craig Kielburger was about your age when he started Free the Children, which is now the largest network of children helping children through education in the world.

Since I've come home from Rwanda, my work has been to make sure that no one forgets what happened there; what I say may not always be popular, but it is the right thing to say. A big part of what I've been trying to do is to educate our youth, and encourage them

**The greatest evils are from within us; and from ourselves, also, we must look for our greatest good.**

*Jeremy Taylor*
*(English Anglican minister and author, 1613–1667)*

to organize and act together. Your voices are important—remember that.

You've already begun learning about things that are happening around the world, and you've already begun asking some tough questions. Tell your friends about it, keep asking questions, and don't be afraid to speak out. Above all, never give up hope. I strongly believe that optimism is the answer. Optimism comes from recognizing that we're in a long-term exercise, and that we're in it together. Global atrocities will take centuries to resolve, but we've been making progress; concepts like human rights, unheard of half a century ago, have moved forward and are gaining ground. We are learning that we, as humans, have a responsibility toward one another. One day, I do believe that the serenity that every human being seeks will be found. Our differences will someday no longer be a source of conflict. Each one of us has a part to play in making that happen.

With best personal regards.
LGen. The Honourable Roméo Dallaire,
Senator

> **A man's true wealth hereafter is the good he does in this world to his fellow man.**
>
> *Muhammad*
> *(Prophet and founder of Islam, 570–632)*

# DEBORAH ELLIS

Deborah Ellis was born on August 1, 1960, in Cochrane, Ontario, and spent the first few years of her life in Moosonee before being raised in Paris, Ontario. While in high school, she became actively involved in the peace movement and became a feminist as a result. She travelled extensively throughout the world, often in dangerous areas, becoming more aware of the issues facing women and children in war-torn countries.

Deb was first published in 1999 and her subsequent novels, including the multi-award-winning Breadwinner trilogy, have focused on the situations faced by children around the world. She has won the Governor General's Award, the Jane Addams Children's Book Award, The Vicky Metcalf Award for a body of work, and the Children's Africana Book Award Honor Book.

Deb continues to spend her life advocating for social justice and making the world a better place. She has donated the vast majority of her royalties to women's and children's causes, and she speaks out, lends her time and support, and continues to tell stories of children marginalized by poverty, war, and illness.

She resides in Simcoe, Ontario.

> I believe that every human mind feels pleasure in doing good to another.
>
> **Thomas Jefferson**
> *(American president, 1743–1836)*

Dear Jo,

It's 2:30 in the morning, and I'm having one of those chopped-up-sleep nights. It seems like a good time to answer your letter. It's somehow easier to get to the point of things when I'm too tired to be pompous and there's nothing on TV but preachers and products.

I do a lot of school talks, and recently spoke at an assembly in a white, well-to-do town. After talking for an hour about the choices we make as human beings, and the long-term destruction and horror of war, one of the teachers came up to me. She said she loved my talk, loved my books, but believes that the only way to have peace is through war. Perhaps she wouldn't feel that way if it were *her* house being bombed, *her* kids being maimed, *her* life being reduced to a few square feet in a refugee camp. She made me glad I spend most of my time talking with children, who are generally too wise to spew that kind of nonsense.

There's a real disconnection in this part of the world between the life we live and

> The difference between what we do and what we are capable of doing would suffice to solve most of the world's problems.
>
> *Mahatma Gandhi*
> *(Indian politician, activist, and visionary, 1869–1948)*

what it costs others to allow us to keep living this life. Much of the chocolate we eat is harvested by child slaves in the cocoa plantations of East Africa. Our clothing is often made in sweatshops in Central America or Asia, where to form a union is to go down a fast track to prison or worse. We are a rich society, easily amused by our televisions and an assortment of ever-emerging electrical gadgets. We're kept busy with consumption and meaningless information, so busy that when our leaders say, "Time to go to war," they expect us to be far too busy to ask why.

The forces that run our world often seem all-powerful, with no way to fight against them, but the very good news is that they don't always win. Workers join together to claim their rights. People who are abused find ways to leave their abusers and bring them to justice. Citizens rise up and reclaim their government from tyrants. And people who could easily do otherwise choose to see the world through clear eyes, and choose to live in a way that does not make things worse.

> By doing good with his money, a man, as it were, stamps the image of God upon it.
>
> *John Rutledge*
> *(American politician and judge, 1739–1800)*

As a kid, your biggest job is to decide what kind of adult you want to be, and to work toward that. You are already asking fundamental questions, and that puts you way ahead of many grown-ups. Make yourself as smart and as strong and as knowledgeable as you can, so that you'll be able to spot when you're being lied to. Know that your life has meaning and value, even when so much around you is telling you otherwise. Know that the people with money and power are just people; they're as foolish as anybody else, and they don't always deserve our allegiance. Know that hope is a verb, one you have to crank up from time to time to keep it alive.

> Acting on a good idea is better than just having a good idea.
>
> **Robert Half**

There are tons of practical ways you can shine your light on the world, and I know that in your search for the truth, you will find the ways that suit you best.

Above all, don't be afraid. In all of my travels, the one thing that gets constantly reaffirmed is that there are many more good people in the world than bad, and they are all on your side.

Thanks for your letter, Jo. It made me feel better. Now, maybe I can get back to sleep.

Best wishes,
Deb

Deborah Ellis

Real integrity is doing the right thing, knowing that nobody's going to know whether you did it or not.

**Oprah Winfrey**
*(American broadcaster and humanitarian, 1954–)*

# DR. NORMAN L. EPSTEIN

Dr. Norman Epstein is a humanitarian who is accomplished in many realms. From emergency room specialist, to author of thought-provoking opinion editorials, to founder and co-chair of Canadians Against Slavery and Torture in Sudan (C.A.S.T.S.), he applies his skills and determination to better mankind.

To be doing good deeds is man's most glorious task.

**Sophocles**
*(Greek playwright, 496 BC–406 BC)*

Norman was born in Sydney, Nova Scotia. He received a B.Sc. from Dalhousie University in Halifax in 1979 and his M.D. from the University of Ottawa in 1985. He worked as a family physician prior to commencing his specialty as an attending emergency department physician, focusing his practice in this area for more than twenty years. Norman has written numerous articles for the *Canadian Journal of Emergency Medicine,* for which he also serves as a peer reviewer, and has served as a teacher of emergency medicine.

Norman has served long-term as a Big Brother and has campaigned and organized programs for the United Jewish Association in Toronto. He has become an impassioned and tireless advocate as the founder and co-chair of C.A.S.T.S., a grassroots coalition of groups and individuals advocating on behalf of the Sudanese who have endured genocide and unspeakable human rights violations. Norman challenges Canadians to not simply witness the atrocities occurring in Sudan but to act morally on behalf of the devastated people there.

Norman is co-founder and one of three directors of Save Darfur Canada (savedarfur canada.org). He lives in Toronto with his wife, Iris, and children, Maor and Chantelle.

**In nothing do men more nearly approach the gods than in doing good to their fellow men.**

*Cicero*

Dr. Norman L. Epstein

Hello Jo,

My father worked as a dentist on Cape Breton Island in eastern Canada, a region of high unemployment and economic hardship, at least by North American standards. He lowered his dental fees well below provincial average for the uninsured, or simply provided care despite knowing he would not be paid. He taught me that all human beings, regardless of race, religion, creed, or income, deserve to be treated equally, with respect and dignity. He taught me to value the height of one's character over the thickness of one's wallet.

My father had an indelible influence on my life—more by example than by preaching. In many ways he was ready to do community or charitable work and imparted the lesson of always giving back to others. It was in large part due to his influence that I decided to become a doctor. He helped me to understand that there is no more noble pursuit in life then helping people.

I heard a presentation by a leader of the Sudanese African Diaspora. He spoke of

It is almost impossible for children and youth to find their way through the seas of life without the guiding light of a good example.

*M. Russell Ballard*
*(American minister and missionary, 1928–)*

slavery in Sudan and how, after witnessing their parents murdered, children are abducted and forced to do hard labour by their masters. Physical beatings and amputations are employed to discipline them. Young girls are abused as concubines—sexual slaves. These children are made to sleep with the animals and are given only scraps of food. They have very little human contact and live a gut-wrenching, miserable existence.

During this presentation, I was shaken enormously by such unspeakable brutality being visited on the most defenseless in society: children. I knew I needed to do something. I co-founded an advocacy group (C.A.S.T.S.— Canadians Against Slavery and Torture in Sudan) that focuses attention on this situation and advocates for change. Co-chairing an advocacy group and speaking up for a particularly oppressed people allows me to help others on a larger scale.

Although I am not devoutly religious, I believe strongly in a major tenet of Judaism: Tikkun Olam, which means mending the world. There is much that is imperfect

> **All good work is done the way ants do things, little by little.**
>
> *Lafcadio Hearn*
> *(Greek author, 1850–1904)*

about our world, where countless people suffer unbearably, and there is no greater purpose than humbly trying to correct these blights on mankind. For me, this is the true meaning of life.

You asked if I thought you could make a difference in the world. One person can start a ripple that creates another ripple, which gives rise to other ripples that eventually build into a wave of change. This is called a grassroots movement. Ending the odious apartheid regime in South Africa started with meetings in churches, synagogues, temples, schools, and living rooms—this is the ripple effect.

You can be a powerful leader who inspires others around a worthy cause. You can stir others to action: letter-writing campaigns and petitions to decision makers, vigils, public rallies, conferences to raise awareness, fundraising, and visiting elected officials alone or in delegations. The sum is greater than its parts, but each part does promote change.

While people worldwide continue to fight against the scourges of famine, disease,

> The good neighbor looks beyond the external accidents and discerns those inner qualities that make all men human and, therefore, brothers.
>
> *Martin Luther King, Jr.*
> *(American activist, visionary, and minister, 1929–1968)*

oppression, and genocide, we have only one fight—against apathy! In our global village, we cannot be indifferent to the suffering of others.

I would like to leave you with the powerful words of Hillel: "If I am not for myself, who will be for me? If I am only for myself, what am I?"

Sincerely,
Dr. Norm Epstein

**If you aren't setting a good example, you're setting a bad one.**

*Unknown*

# DR. MARC GARNEAU (PH.D)

Dr. Marc Garneau was born on February 23, 1949 in Quebec City. His spirit for adventure was demonstrated early in his life when he crossed the Atlantic in a 59-foot yawl with 12 other crewmen in both the summers of 1969 and 1970. Marc Garneau graduated from the Royal Military College in Kingston Ontario in 1970 with a degree in Engineering Physics and followed this in 1973 with a doctorate degree in Electrical Engineering from the Imperial College of Science and Technology in London England.

Dr. Garneau began working in naval engineering for the Canadian Forces in 1974 and after many achievements and an impressive technical career he attained promotion to Captain in 1986. Dr. Garneau was one of six potential Canadian astronauts selected in December 1983, and after specified training he flew in three shuttle missions in 1984, 1996 and in 2000, logging over 677 hours in space. He completed training that qualified him for assignment as a Mission Specialist. Dr. Garneau was appointed President of the Canadian Space Agency, a position which he held from 2001 to 2005.

"Service to others is the rent you pay for your room here on Earth."

**Muhammad Ali**
*(American boxer, 1942)*

Amongst his many honours, Dr. Garneau was awarded the NASA Exceptional Service Medal in 1997; was made a Companion of the Order of Canada in 2003 and was named Chancellor of Carleton University the same year.

Dr. Garneau is married and the father of 4 children. He enjoys flying, scuba diving, tennis and squash. He travels and lectures about his experiences, highlighting the importance of continued space exploration in the 21st century.

**Dr. Marc Garneau**

Hello Jo,

I've thought a lot about your questions, Jo, especially the first one. I gave myself the challenge of trying to find the simplest possible answer. It's not a complete answer but I hope it helps.

Humans, like animals, have a basic instinct for survival, and although you may not personally feel that you are driven by this instinct, it is at work in each of us and plays a role in our behaviour. For instance, it sometimes makes us angry. The challenge is to bring that anger under control so that we only use it in a positive manner.

Let's look at an example. Anger can be a positive force if you are facing a mountain lion that wants to kill you. First, you experience fear and that can lead to a form of anger. That anger mobilizes all of your strength and reflexes to give you the best chance of survival. But anger can also be a very negative force in our lives.

We have all experienced the negative side of anger. I know I get angry sometimes. After it happens, I feel badly about it. I wish I hadn't lost control of myself. I wish I had used reason instead of anger. But it happens and anger is responsible for many of the bad things people do to other people.

Let's look at it more closely.

*What makes me angry in the first place?*

It's usually because I don't agree with what someone has said or done. Most of the time, I don't get angry even if I don't agree. I tell myself, it's not worth getting angry about. But sometimes, if I feel strongly about something, I get angry. Anger is a powerful emotion.

*How do I behave when I'm angry?*

When I'm angry, my emotions take over and I say or do things I would not normally say or do. I don't think clearly because I'm controlled by my anger. This is when bad things happen and that includes everything from small fights to full-scale wars.

*How do I feel when it's over?*

"Nobody made a greater mistake than he who did nothing because he could do only a little."

**Edmond Burke**
*(British author and politician, 1729–1797)*

I always feel badly after I've been angry. I feel disappointed with myself because I know I said or did things that hurt someone's feelings or that were just plain mean.

*Is there a way to avoid anger?*

Yes, but it takes self-discipline and maturity. Most of all, it requires "breathing room." What I mean by that is taking the time to reflect on what others have said or done. When I see myself beginning to get angry, I try to give myself a "time-out" so that I can allow myself to think clearly. 99% of the time, I no longer feel angry after that "cool down period."

*Do I have a role model to follow?*

Is there an example in our World of a great human being who knew how to avoid anger and violence? For me, there is. That person was the Mahatma Gandhi, someone who was able to express his opinions and achieve his goals (India's independence) without resorting to violence. A model I am trying to follow. Sadly, Gandhi himself was the victim of violence when he was assassinated.

Little by little a person becomes good, as a water pot is filled by drops of water.

**Buddha**
*(Founder of Buddhism, 560 BC –486 BC)*

I have spoken of our survival instinct and how this sometimes leads to anger. However, bad things also happen in this world for reasons other than anger. For example, simple greed when someone wants something that belongs to someone else. Again, there is a link to survival. We want more than we need because it will improve our chances of survival. Or indifference, when someone doesn't care enough about someone else's suffering to reach out to them. Here, we feel we don't want to risk our own survival by helping someone else.

I was fortunate to be the first Canadian astronaut when I flew into space. To leave the earth behind and to enter space was an incredible human achievement and showed what we are, as a species, capable of doing. This action was the product of the work of literally tens of thousands of people, each working on their individual part, to make the sum even greater than the parts. It showed the potential of mankind to rise above mere instincts, to work together. From space I looked down and saw the entire world beneath me. I became even more aware of the shared world we live in. We are all on the same space ship and need to work together. Humans have come a long way from their days as cave dwellers. Today, their challenge is to put compassion and generosity ahead of anger, greed and indifference. It's an extremely difficult challenge but it begins with each of us. It begins with you.

Sincerely,
Marc Garneau

There is no higher religion than human service. To work for the common good is the greatest creed.

**Woodrow Wilson**
*(American president, 1856–1924)*

# JANE GOODALL

In the summer of 1960, 26-year-old Jane Goodall arrived on the shore of Lake Tanganyika in East Africa to study the area's chimpanzee population.

Although it was unheard of for a woman to venture into the wilds of the African forest, the trip meant the fulfillment of Jane Goodall's childhood dream. Jane's work in Tanzania would prove more successful than anyone had imagined.

At first, the Gombe chimps fled whenever they saw Jane. But she persisted, watching from a distance with binoculars, and gradually the chimps allowed her closer. One day in October 1960 she saw chimps David Graybeard and Goliath strip leaves off twigs to fashion tools for fishing termites from a nest. Scientists thought humans were the only species to make tools, but here was evidence to the contrary.

In 1977, Jane founded the Jane Goodall Institute for Wildlife Research, Education and Conservation to provide ongoing support for field research on wild chimpanzees. Today, the mission of the Jane Goodall Institute is to advance the power of individuals to take informed and compassionate action to improve the environment for all living things.

A journey of a thousand miles begins with a single step.

*Lao-tzu*
*(Chinese philosopher and father of Taoism,*
*604 BC–531 BC)*

Dr. Goodall's scores of honors include the medal of Tanzania, the National Geographic Society's Hubbard Medal, Japan's prestigious Kyoto Prize, the Prince of Asturias Award for Technical and Scientific Research 2003, the Benjamin Franklin Medal in Life Science, and the Ghandi/King Award for Nonviolence. In April 2002 Secretary-General Annan named Dr. Goodall a United Nations "Messenger of Peace." In 2003, Queen Elizabeth II named Dr. Goodall a Dame of the British Empire, the equivalent of a knighthood.

Today, Jane Goodall spends much of her time lecturing, sharing her message of hope for the future and encouraging young people to make a difference in their world.

For more Information:

**www.rootsandshoots.org**

Dear Jo,

Thank you for your letter. Your questions are ones I have often asked myself, and I'll try to respond as best I can.

The question "why do people act the way they do?" is a difficult one for anyone to answer, regardless of age or background. I was only about nine years old when the first images documenting the atrocities of the Holocaust were made public. I remember climbing a tree and sitting by myself, thinking and thinking for an extremely long time, struggling with what I'd seen. I wondered how a just God could allow such unfathomable horrors to happen.

> He who waits to do a great deal of good at once, will never do anything.
>
> **Samuel Johnson**
> *(English writer, 1709–1784)*

People tend to say, "God works in mysterious ways, his wonders to perform," or that we can't really understand the larger intentions of the universe. Some people explain suffering through the concept of karma, and say that one accumulates wisdom over hundreds of years of evolution of the human soul. Others answer these questions in non-religious ways; for them, the answers are found in sociobiology.

I don't know if I can answer that question for you, because I can't answer it for myself. We simply don't understand, and all we can do is try to use our own lives to make things better, to do everything we can. It's a challenge for us: what can we do to reduce suffering? What can we do to make the world a better place? How can we do it together?

It is easy to be overwhelmed by feelings of hopelessness as we look around the world. Terrible pollution is ravaging the environment, the balance of nature is disturbed, and we are destroying our beautiful planet. There are fears of new epidemics for which there will be no drugs, and rather than fight the cause, we torture millions of animals in the name of medical progress.

Yet, there are many signs of hope. Along a lakeshore in Tanzania, for example, villagers are planting trees where all the previous ones had disappeared. The women are taking more control over their lives; once they become better educated, birth rates begin to drop. And the children are being taught about the dire effects of habitat destruction. I've seen

Avoid envy, for envy devours good deeds just as fire devours fuel.

**Muhammad**
*(Prophet and founder of Islam, 570–632)*

how their community has shifted from desperation to optimism.

We are at a pivotal moment in our planet's history. Only by taking action now can we move it away from the brink of destruction.

One way you can make a difference is by joining Roots & Shoots. Roots & Shoots began in 1991 with a small group of concerned young people who came to me to discuss a range of problems that concerned them: pollution in the city, deforestation in the mountains, and the future of the region's animals. These motivated young people wanted to learn more and, most importantly, were willing to take action.

The first Roots & Shoots project was local: educating villagers about more humane treatment of chickens at home and in the region's markets. It was a small program, but encompassed all of the hallmarks of what makes Roots & Shoots so special even today: youth-driven projects fuelled by knowledge, compassion, and action.

> **For those to whom much is given, much is required.**
>
> *John F. Kennedy*
> *(American president, 1917–1963)*

Today, the Roots & Shoots network branches out across the globe, with tens of thousands of young people in almost a hundred countries. By connecting youth of all ages who share a common desire to help make our world a better place, it fosters a fun, flexible, and supportive environment in which young people and adults alike come together to share ideas and inspiration, implement successful community service projects, and participate in special events and global campaigns.

By getting involved in Roots & Shoots, you can meet other children who share the same concerns as you do, as well as caring, informed adults who will try to answer some of your questions. It's about making positive change happen—for our communities, for animals, and for the environment. And it all starts with you.

There are no easy answers to life's most challenging questions. The only thing we, as concerned individuals, can do is keep trying to reach out to others and never stop trying to improve this world we share.

> A tree is known by its fruit; a man by his deeds. A good deed is never lost.
>
> **Saint Basil the Great**
> *(Religious leader, 329–379)*

Great change can begin with individual actions. I wish you good luck in this journey.

Yours,
Jane Goodall

Jane Goodall

**He is not great who is not greatly good.**

***William Shakespeare***
*(English playwright, 1564–1616)*

# RICK HANSEN

Rick Hansen was born August 26th, 1957, in Port Alberni and grew up in Fort St. John, Abbotsford, and Williams Lake, B.C. A natural athlete, he was very passionate about fishing and sports.

One day in August 1973, Rick and his friend Don Alder were riding in the back of a pickup truck, returning home from a week-long fishing trip. The truck went off the steep, winding road, and Rick and Don were thrown out of the back. Rick sustained a spinal cord injury and would never walk again. He was paralyzed from the waist down.

After seven months, Rick returned home from rehabilitation in Vancouver. Slowly, he learned how to deal with his new life, found a way to keep fishing, and with the encouragement of his volleyball coach, stayed involved in sports. He discovered wheelchair basketball and other sports, set new goals for his life . . . and began to make new dreams.

Between 1979 and 1984, Rick turned his focus to track, winning nineteen international wheelchair marathons, the world title four times, and nine gold medals at the 1982 Pan Am Games. He won a gold and silver medal at the 1984 Paralympic Summer Games in Stoke

**The best way to keep good intentions from dying is to execute them.**

*Unknown*

Mandeville, and a gold, silver, and bronze at the 1980 Paralympic Summer Games in Arnhem, Holland. He also competed for Canada in the 1984 Olympic Games in track, as an exhibition sport, and was the first person to break the two-hour time in a wheelchair marathon.

While Rick was a celebrated international athlete, he was also committed to making a difference in the lives of others. Combining his passions, athletic ability and vision, he pushed his wheelchair out of Vancouver, B.C, on March 21, 1985, to set out on a journey that would make history.

The Man In Motion World Tour was fuelled by two big dreams: to make communities more accessible and inclusive and to raise funds for spinal cord injury research. Every day, Rick completed the equivalent of three marathons— through all kinds of terrain, in all kinds of weather.

The journey took Rick and his team through thirty-four countries: they crossed the United States, wheeled through Britain and Europe, the Middle East, New Zealand, Australia, and the Far East before returning to North America, going from Miami to New York, then back to Canada.

On May 22, 1987, thousands of people lined the streets to welcome Rick and the team home.

> But the angels who examine him in the grave will ask, "What good deeds hast thou sent before thee?"
>
> **Muhammad**
> (Prophet and founder of Islam, 570–632)

The tour raised $26 million for spinal cord injury research, rehabilitation, and sport. In 1988, he established the Rick Hansen Foundation and today, as president and CEO, remains committed to making communities more accessible and inclusive for people with spinal cord injuries, and accelerating the search for a cure. Through Rick's leadership, the Foundation has generated more than $200 million for spinal cord injury–related programs and initiatives. Rick has received the Companion of the Order of Canada, and the Order of British Columbia, initiated National Access Awareness Week in Canada, was inducted into Canada's Walk of Fame, is honorary chair for a number of provincial and national advisory councils on disabilities, and holds twelve honorary degrees from Canadian universities.

Money—it is powerful for good if divinely used.

**George Macdonald**
*(Scottish novelist, 1824–1905)*

Rick Hansen

Dear Jo,

Thank you for writing to me. You have asked some very difficult but important questions and, though I'm not sure I have the answers, I will do my best to respond.

Life can be very confusing sometimes—even for grown-ups. It seems unfair that so many people live in poverty, tragedy, and sadness, while others live in communities where they are respected and have roofs over their heads, food on the table, and friends and families who love them. What's even more heart-breaking, as you have said, is the way that some people treat others.

I believe that when people are inconsiderate or unkind to one another, they are usually driven by fear, ignorance, or a lack of knowledge. Fear is a powerful force that can make people act in very negative, hurtful ways, causing them to do things that they would not normally do.

Fear can be conquered, though, through awareness and knowledge, by learning about different people, lifestyles, and beliefs.

No act of kindness, no matter how small, is ever wasted.

**Aesop**
*(Turkish or Egyptian storyteller and philosopher, 620 BC –560 BC)*

Knowledge gives you the power to see that there is often very little truth behind our fears. It offers you the ability to accept others for who they are and allows you to embrace them, rather than judge them for being different. Knowledge is the root of acceptance, the motivation for diversity, and the force that can end the cruelty going on around the world.

> We ought to do our neighbour all the good we can. If you do good, good will be done to you.
>
> *Pilpay*
> *(Persian fables)*

I learned about these things years ago when something happened to me that changed my life. You see, when I was just a young man, not much older than you, I was injured in a car accident. My spine was broken and I was told that I would never walk again. Since then, I have had the opportunity to meet all kinds of people. Some have judged me and treated me unfairly, but most have been supportive, caring, helpful, and kind. They have encouraged me to pursue my dreams, believed in my ability, and understood that being in a wheelchair doesn't mean I'm not capable of great things.

Throughout my life I have faced many challenges, from which I have learned that anybody, big or small, can make a difference.

There is an immense power in the human spirit, and the ability to help others lies within all of us. Whether you're a leader or a follower, whether you're on the back end or the front end of a team, it doesn't matter. If you understand an issue, are motivated and committed to finding a solution, you will make a difference.

I hope I have helped to answer your questions, Jo. I will leave you with one final thought, in the hopes that it will help you in your pursuit to improve the lives of others: If you believe in a dream and have the courage to try, great things can be accomplished. Anything is possible.

With respect and admiration,
Rick Hansen

**But it is part of a good man to do great and noble deeds though he risks everything in doing them.**

*Plutarch*
*(Greek philosopher, 45–125)*

# BEN HEPPNER

Ben Heppner was born on January 14, 1956, in Murrayville, British Columbia, and raised in Dawson Creek, B.C. He studied music at the University of British Columbia, and his first major break came in 1979 when he won the Canadian Broadcasting Corporation Talent Festival. He has since been recognized worldwide as the finest dramatic tenor performing today. Ben won the 1988 Metropolitan Opera auditions, has received numerous awards, such as Juno Awards (1996, 2002) and Grammy Awards (1998, 2001), and was named as an Officer of the Order of Canada. Ben is a celebrated recording artist and performs around the world, often undertaking the most challenging and demanding of roles.

Ben is a husband and father and resides in Toronto. He is a deeply committed Christian who lends his voice and support to numerous charities and causes.

For more information: **www.heppner.com**

> **None but a good man is really a living man, and the more good any man does, the more he really lives.**
>
> *Herman Melville*
> *(American author, 1819–1891)*

**Ben Heppner**

Dear Jo,

As you have noticed when speaking with your teachers, parents, and grandparents, it is also difficult for older people to answer the tough questions you have asked about unfairness, cruelty, tragedy, and hatred in the world. As you point out, I am an older person and, as you know, we don't have all the answers, but out of respect for your important questions and the time you took to write to me, let me try to put down a few thoughts for you.

I am an artist—a singer of classical songs—not any kind of expert in what makes people hate or act unkindly to one another. What I'd like to do, though, is tell you about the things it seems are all too easy to overlook in the search for answers.

> Look within. Within is the fountain of good, and it will ever bubble up, if thou wilt ever dig.
>
> **Marcus Aurelius**
> *(Roman emperor, 121–180)*

What happened to me, Jo, is that I learned the stories of my faith, particularly the stories Jesus told (we call them parables), and they made a huge impression on me. We must do what we can to help the sick, to encourage the faint of heart, to comfort those who grieve and who suffer, to visit those in prison, to support the poor—*and not just talk about doing so.* We must strive to be humble, to recognize our own frailty, and to ask God for help in this world. And, yes, we must do what we can to act justly, to love fully, to share with an open heart, to bring forth beauty into this world like light into a darkened cave. The stories all point in that direction.

Fortunately, religions tell us about love, mercy, joy, and forgiveness, and about our obligations to others as well. To be humble, to do justice, and to love rather than hate or be selfish are the central insights of religion. Of course, we don't always live according to what our faiths tell us to do, but we at least have a guide that those without such insights might not possess as easily or see as clearly before them. So, the answer to your first question depends on how we view why people act the way they do—is our search going to be enriched by religious, spiritual, and philosophical insights in addition to science? I think it should be and that, depending on what we believe (and we all believe *something,* whether we know it or not), we will find explanations to the world around us. You need to look for something that offers the best explanation for human conduct (positive and negative) and base your beliefs on that as you move through life; we all do.

All of your questions show that there is something in your heart, and perhaps in the hearts of many, that rejects certain things you find unfair and difficult to explain. That is a good thing, for it shows that you are not blind to the troubles of others in this world. In fact, concern can lead us to compassion, and compassion comes from love.

In a gentle way, you can shake the world.

**Mahatma Gandhi**
*(Indian politician, activist, and visionary, 1869–1948)*

We cannot explain in logical terms why we would love, why we see caring and self-sacrifice as better than selfishness and the sacrifice of others. That's because it is not simply a question of logic! This is where I think beauty, art, and faith come in.

You want to know whether one kid can make a difference. First of all, you are not just "one kid" but part of a network of people. Your family, your community, your place of worship, and your associations (school, sports, music, and clubs) all connect you with other people. It is through group action that so much good (as well as evil) has been done in the world. In fact, one of today's big challenges is to overcome the sense of isolation that so many people have and to realize that we, as human beings, exist in relation to one another, whether we know it or not. You can assist in raising this awareness by how you live your life. Your questions suggest that you are already thinking of others.

You can make a difference by learning to think about what your gifts and interests are and how you can use them to shine light into the world. Sounds simple, doesn't it? Well, it is not, but that is the work of your life—and of all our lives, in one way or another.

Your questions are full of faith that things *can* be better; if it were not so, why would you—why would any of us—ask these questions? To understand that it is better to light a single candle than to curse the darkness is recognition that there *is* light and that it is stronger than darkness, no matter how difficult that may be to believe from time to time.

As you grow older, I hope you continue to keep your questions vivid and before you so that you will be one of those people who

> **Be not simply good; be good for something.**
>
> *Henry David Thoreau*
> *(American writer and philosopher, 1817–1862)*

encourages others, who offers hope rather than despair, comfort rather than cynicism, and kind words rather than harsh words. For on that awareness and that choice to "do good" stands the future of our lives together and the hope for a better world. Your questions point in that direction. Thank you for asking them. Forgive me that my responses are not so much answers as suggestions; but they are the suggestions I was given by those who loved and nurtured me and they are the things that guide me as I try, in my own way, to bring beauty into the world through my life and my music. We musicians, like all artists, are channels of a beauty we do not create, and we know the joy of inspiration as well.

May you find your role as a channel of love and beauty, Jo, and may you look for inspiration in your own life and sow the seeds of inspiration in the lives of others.

Sincerely,
Ben Heppner

The discovery of what is true and the practice of that which is good are the two most important objects of philosophy.

**Voltaire**
*(French dramatist and philosopher, 1694–1778)*

# KOFI HOPE

> The best place to find a helping hand is at the end of your own arm.
>
> *Swedish proverb*

Kofi Hope was born in 1983 in Mississauga, Ontario. His interest in social justice and community activism first took flight during his high school years. He was the director of the Erin Mills Youth Outreach Program, a youth drop-in and literacy program run out of Erin Mills United Church, and subsequently ran the United Church of Canada's Youth Connections program, designed to help increase the capacity of the church to work with black, Aboriginal, and Asian/South Asian youth in social justice settings. Kofi is the founder and chairman of the Black Youth Coalition Against Violence, a group dedicated to fostering empowerment of black youth and advocating for them around issues of violence. He served as president of the University of Toronto Black Students' Association and graduated in 2007 with a B.A., majoring in political science with a minor in African studies and world religions.

Kofi was awarded the prestigious Rhodes Scholarship and is currently attending Oxford University in England, where he is working on his doctorate degree in Politics.

For more information:
**www.bycav.com**
**www.united-church.ca**

Hey Jo,

Thanks for the letter. My name is Kofi and you could call me a community activist. I just finished university and I do a lot of work with other young people in tough situations. You asked some really good questions and I wanted to talk about the first one: why do people treat each other badly? Well, it's a tough one, but I would say let's ask a different question. Instead, ask: why don't people do all the good things they could do? Because I see hope in the world. We currently have the potential to solve global warming, to cure cancer, to stop wars. There are more than six billion human beings alive and each one is tremendously gifted whether in poetry, mathematics, sports, raising children, listening to others' problems, designing buildings, teaching . . . the list goes on forever. If we had a world in which all of these people were able to use their gifts for good, I believe it would be pretty close to perfect.

The problem is this. Today's societies do not allow every person to live to his or her full potential. Unfortunately, I would say that the world we have today stops the

**Do not wait for extraordinary circumstances to do good; try to use ordinary situations.**

*Jean Paul Richter*
*(German writer,*
*1763–1825)*

majority of people from achieving their potential. That's the great injustice of our world, and it's why people talk about working toward social justice. But what is this social justice thing?

There was a boy I knew named O'Neal. He was amazing at math and a wiz with electronics. He could repair your Walkman by himself, if you asked. But he had a rough childhood: his father abandoned him, he had to leave his home country of Barbados, and even worse, he came to a place (Canada) where people treated him differently because of the colour of his skin. Further, after he came here his mother had to struggle to put food on the table and wasn't around much. They lived in a poor area, one that was run-down and filled with guys hanging out on the corners all day, selling drugs and getting into fights. The strange thing was, these same guys seemed to be the only people in the neighbourhood who had money or respect.

O'Neal knew he was smart and that, if he worked hard, he could be an engineer. But life was just too much for him. Maybe it was poverty, his family life, racism, the fact that

> Every one of us needs to show how much we care for each other and, in the process, care for ourselves.
>
> *Diana, Princess of Wales*
> *(Member of the British royal family, 1961–1997)*

teachers never seemed to believe in him, or that he struggled to find a job. Whatever it was, he started to give up on himself. He decided to be like the guys on the corner, to join a gang, to sell drugs, to carry a gun. He saw it as the fastest way to become somebody, to feel good about himself, to show that he had worth. All anyone wants is to feel is that they are special. But this was the wrong way to go about it, and soon his world came crashing down.

This is a story I have seen repeated too many times. Situations stop people from being able to share their gifts; even worse, they sometimes push people to do evil instead. I believe that we all have an amazing light shining inside us, but sometimes the world throws so much crap at us it gets buried so deep that no one can see it anymore. For example, I read that there are more than 200 million children all over the world who will never get to finish school because they can't afford eyeglasses. Just think of all the smart people you know with glasses. Think of all the gifts we are losing just because of this one problem.

**The purpose of human life is to serve, and to show compassion and the will to help others.**

*Albert Schweitzer*
*(German doctor and humanitarian, 1875–1965)*

Think about all of the great scientists, doctors, politicians, and architects you have read about in history class. Now, realize that for almost all of history, women—50 percent of our species—have been prevented from playing important roles in all of those fields due to discrimination. For thousands of years, we have stopped half of the most talented people around from ever having the chance to contribute to those professions. Think of all we have lost. Today, experts say that things are better, but the facts are still scary: women own only 1 percent of the world's property, and 70 percent of people living in the worst poverty on earth are women! These same results have been replicated many times, in different situations, for people who have been discriminated against because of their colour, religion, age, country of origin, language, or disabilities.

The more I learned about social justice, whether at university or in real life, the more I realized that there were only two things I could do: sit at home and complain about it, or go out and do something. I was confronted with just this choice two summers ago, while reading newspaper headlines about gun violence in Toronto. Each story I read seemed to be about another black kid being killed. The whole thing bothered me—where were the black kids I knew, the ones volunteering at community centres, running organizations, tutoring, and being positive? Our voices seemed never to be heard. So, I decided to do something. I organized a meeting with a bunch of other student leaders I knew. We started to sell bracelets and posters, calling for other black youth to come together and be proud of doing something positive in their community. We went to events and meetings, telling people that this violence in our city was the result of poverty, lack of jobs, community breakdown, and racism. We didn't need more police on the streets; we needed more support for kids like O'Neal. As we became better organized, we ended up meeting all of the same politicians I had seen in the news and getting ourselves on the front cover of the paper. A few months later, we organized a summit for 650 young people to come together to show that black youth in the city did care. The work continues today.

**Kindness is an inner desire that makes us want to do good things even if we do not get anything in return. It is the joy of our life to do them.**

*Emanuel Swedenborg (Swedish scientist and philosopher, 1688–1772)*

It's work we all have to take a part in. We have a society today that favours stuff—SUVs, jewellery, big-screen TVs—over people. A society in which it's more important to be thin and beautiful than to be kind and caring. In which people here die from eating too much, while people in the rest of the world die from not having access to enough food. The world got this way because, for too long, a few people with power and wealth made decisions for everyone, and the majority had no say. Now it's time to change things, but we all have to step up, especially young people. This country, this world, is ours just as much as it belongs to adults, and we have a responsibility to work to improve it.

But, Jo, sometimes I almost lose hope. People do so much evil all over the world, it can make you feel that there is no point in trying. When this happens, I look to my faith in God to keep me strong and I think of my role models: Jesus, Gandhi, Martin Luther King Jr., and Malcolm X. I also think of the individuals I have touched, like Christophe. He was a kid at the youth program I ran. He used to be a terror: biting kids, stealing bikes, and teasing. Over the

> **Service to others is the rent you pay for your room here on earth.**
>
> *Muhammad Ali*
> *(American heavyweight boxing champion, 1942–)*

years, the staff kept supporting him—we never gave up on him—and I watched as he grew into an articulate young man. This year, he joined a film group we started, and ended up starring in a movie that talked about issues in his community. It's these things that help me keep the faith.

Peace,
Kofi Hope

Kofi Hope

# LYNN JOHNSTON

Lynn was born in Collingwood, Ontario and raised in British Columbia. She trained as an artist at the Vancouver School of Art, her main interest being animation. Unable to obtain work as an animator she became a medical artist at McMaster University in Hamilton.

Expecting her first child she was challenged by her obstetrician to create drawings for the ceiling above the examination tables, and during her eight months of regular visits she created over 80 comics, her view of pregnancy. These were published in a book called *David, We're Pregnant*. Subsequently she created two more highly successful books, Hi *Mom, Hi Dad,* and *Do They Ever Grow Up?*

Lynn was approached and offered an opportunity to create a daily comic strip. This comic, For Better or Worse, was based on the members of her family, and now appears in over 2,000 papers in Canada, the United States and 20 other countries and has been translated into eight languages. There have been 35 books based on her comic strip.

Lynn has consistently demonstrated the ability to use a few panels and a few words to create laughter, tears, provoke thought, and

> Human behaviour must be guided by a higher principle. Practicality has its place, but only within a framework of values, which all men of good will share.
>
> **King Hussein**
> *(Jordanian political and religious leader, 1935–1999)*

inspire, as millions of people have been part of the lives of her created family, following them in their live passages as they continue in theirs. The magic of her comic is that while it has made us all laugh it has also dealt with important issues, raised awareness of sensitive issues in a sensitive manner, broken taboos and created meaningful dialogue.

Lynn has received dozens of honours and awards, including an Order of Canada, a Gemini Award, a Reuben Award, an Order of Mariposa, Comic of the Year, Inkpot Award, and is a member of the Female Cartoonists Hall of Fame. She is also a tireless contributor to community good including supporting the Farley Foundation (which finances medical care for pets belonging to seniors and people with disabilities), the Raising Readers program, and the Hospital Foundation of North Bay.

**Lynn Johnston**

Dear Jo,

When I was five a burglar broke into our modest house. He took some jewellery and our television. It wasn't much, but we were not well off and the loss was awful. It was a cruel thing to do to a nice family. I asked my mother if there were more good people on earth than bad ones and she said she sincerely hoped so—but, she really didn't know! She said that no matter what happened to us, we had to always be considerate of and care for others. Honesty, modesty, generosity were words my parents used often and we learned to give everyone a chance—even if we were different colours, even if we spoke different languages or were of different faiths. Everyone was equal and deserving of respect—unless their behaviour proved otherwise.

All of the questions you are asking, I have been asking too—ever since I was very young. I have wondered: why are people mean to each other, why are we so selfish, why do we lie, cheat, steal and commit awful crimes against each other?! I say "we" because we are all guilty. We all do cruel things and cruel things are done to us—it's "human nature," somehow, to assert ourselves by bullying others.

The closer I get to death, the more I wonder about "human nature" because, in the end, this need to have the most power, the most money, and the most attention leads . . . nowhere! We can't take any material things with us when we die. We leave behind all the things we owned—and we leave something infinitely more important than possessions—we leave our reputation. Will we be remembered with pride and affection? Or will those we leave behind be glad we're gone forever?

Some people go down in history for the good they have done—and others, for the crimes they have committed. Human nature gives us the power to choose between good and evil and the intelligence to predict the results of our actions. I have always wondered why war was necessary when we are all so capable of concise communication. I have always wondered why a planet that could provide food, shelter and amenities for all sustains only a portion of its inhabitants.

"Our deeds determine us, as much as we determine our deeds."

*George Eliot*
*(British novelist, 1818–1890)*

Even with this good upbringing, I was and am guilty still of unkindness to others and I wonder why. Human Nature. As much as we laud our superiority over the animals, we are animals, nonetheless. I believe we are animals with many gifts, qualities, abilities and infinite potential. We are still evolving. We discover new things every day about life, death and the universe, but we don't really know why we are here!

Maybe it's to learn the biggest lesson of all. Maybe we're here to break free, go beyond the restrictions of "human nature" and learn to focus on everything around us, before we serve ourselves.

Until we can all rise above our basic human instincts, until we can all stop saying "me first," your very important questions will remain unanswered.

But, Jo—don't ever stop asking!!

Sincerely,
Lynn Johnston

# CRAIG KIELBURGER

Craig was born on December 12 1982 in Thornhill, Ontario. At age twelve he learned about the life and death of another twelve-year-old, Iqhal Masih of Pakistan. Iqhal, who was sold into slavery in a carpet factory, escaped and spoke out against the working conditions, the slavery of children. For taking this stand to defend the rights of children he was murdered. Craig, along with some of his school friends, created Free The Children to fight child labour around the world.

Free The Children has become the largest network of children helping children through education and development and has impacted on more than one million young people in more than forty-five countries around the world. The primary goals of the organization are to free children from poverty and exploitation and to help young people understand their power to make positive changes in the world.

Craig has received numerous awards and honours including the Nelson Mandela Human Rights Award, the Roosevelt Freedom medal, the Governor General's Medal of Meritorious Service, and was named as a Companion to the Order of Canada.

"When the story of these times gets written, we want it to say that we did all we could, and it was more than anyone could have imagined."

**Bono**
*(Irish rock star and social activist, 1960–)*

He is a tireless advocate for children's rights, a social activist, a leadership specialist, author and speaker, who travels the world to continue the mission that he started when he was twelve.

For more information:
**www.freethechildren.com**

You shall love your neighbour as yourself.

*Jesus*
*(6 B.C.–36 A.D.)*

Craig Kielburger

Hi Jo,

I'm sitting in the Maasai Mara, the breath-taking land of Western Kenya home to wild lions, elephants and giraffes. The sun has just set over the hills and the stars are slowly coming out. The scenery is beautiful, but it's a place where many children don't go to school because they can't afford books or uniforms. Instead they walk for hours a day to collect water from the local river. It's dirty and it makes them sick, but that's all they have. There are no jobs for their parents, so there isn't any money for food. Life is not easy here.

I've just read your letter. In it you asked some very important questions, ones I ask myself every day. Why do people like the ones in the Maasai Mara have to live with "so little?" I think it's because our modern, hectic society focuses on getting ahead of one another, on competing and winning, no matter what the cost is to other people. So some people have forgotten the importance of helping others— whether it's in their own neighbourhoods, in their country or in another part of the world. Gratitude, empathy and community lose out because we worry too much about what makes us different from one another, not what makes us the same. As I sometimes say, today's world is centred too much on "me" and not enough on "we."

I was first moved to help at the age of twelve. One morning I opened the newspaper to read the comics, but something on the front page caught my attention. It was a picture of a young boy wearing a bright red vest, his arm raised in the air. The headline said, "Battled Child Labour, Boy, 12, Murdered." I had never heard of child labour before, but I read on. The boy's name was Iqbal Masih. He was sold into slavery at the age of four and forced to help make carpets in Pakistan. Years later he escaped and became an international child rights activist, travelling the world and speaking about his life. But the attention he drew angered the wrong people, and Iqbal was shot dead while riding his bike. I was so shocked. How could a boy the same age as me have to live through so much? I tore the article out of the paper and brought it to school. Then I showed it to my class and asked who wanted to help me fight child labour. Eleven people raised their hands and Free The Children was born.

Since then, the organization has become the world's largest network of children helping children through education, with more than one million young people in forty-five countries. Every day I meet youth who are making a difference, some by collecting cans of food for the homeless and volunteering at local community centres, others by travelling to a developing country to help build a school. Together, they have helped build more than 450 schools in 16 countries. I was excited to read your letter because it showed that you are on the right track. You are learning and asking questions. Knowledge is power, so learn everything you can about an issue that concerns you and speak to others with a similar passion. Build a team of people who share your goal of a better tomorrow and take the time help someone who needs it. Every action makes a difference!

Good luck to you, Jo. Thank you for writing. Remember the words of one of my heroes, Mahatma Gandhi: "You must be the change you want to see in the world."

Your friend,
Craig Kielburger

There are people in the world so hungry that God cannot appear to them except in the form of bread.

**Mahatma Gandhi**
*(Indian politician, activist, and visionary, 1869–1948)*

# ROY MACGREGOR

Roy MacGregor was born in the small village of Whitney, Ontario, in 1948, and raised in Huntsville, both on the boundaries of Algonquin Park. His grandfather was chief park ranger, his mother was born there, and his father worked there as a logger for his entire life.

Roy is a nationally acclaimed newspaper columnist and reporter, has written for magazines, and has created non-fiction books as well as novels for both adults and children. His writing has led to four National Magazine Awards, two ACTRA Awards for television, nine nominations for the National Newspaper Award (winning twice), and the U.S. Rutstrum Award for best wilderness book. As well, he has been nominated for the Governor General's Award and shortlisted for numerous other awards, including the Trillium Book Award and the Stephen Leacock Memorial Medal for Humour, and has won Young Readers Awards in both Manitoba and Saskatchewan. In September 2005, he was made an Officer of the Order of Canada. He is described in the citation as one of Canada's "most-gifted storytellers."

Roy is the author of more than thirty-five books, twenty-two of them in the internationally

> Those who do good as opportunity offers are sowing seed all the time, and they need not doubt the harvest.
>
> *Unknown*

successful Screech Owls Mystery series for young readers. His most recent book is *Canadians: A Portrait of the Country and Its People,* a study of the country he has written about and travelled throughout for more than thirty years.

Roy lives in Kanata, Ontario, with Ellen. They have four children: Kerry, Christine, Jocelyn, and Gordon.

Roy MacGregor

A pessimist sees the difficulty in any opportunity; an optimist sees the opportunity in every difficulty.

*Winston Churchill*
*(British prime minister and orator, 1874–1965)*

Dear Jo,

As the father of four energetic children, I have noticed that kids always ask the best questions. I'm not just talking about "Are we *there* yet?" but about the absolutely impossible-to-answer questions a child will ask merely by unleashing his or her curiosity. Like most parents, I can recall driving in the car and having the ultimate question come from the back seat: "Dad, did God create everything?"

"Of course," the parent responds, not thinking for a moment about either question or answer, more likely thinking of where he's going or what she has to do next on the endless list that is parenting.

"Well, then, *who* created God?"

Sorry, but there are some questions—no, there are a lot of questions—I simply cannot answer. I have no answers. I don't really think anyone does. But I also happen to believe that one of the truly magnificent beauties of being alive is that every once in a while you are struck by pure awe. You simply cannot know

**Well done is better than well said.**

*Benjamin Franklin*
*(American scientist, inventor, and politician, 1706–1790)*

some things, including the future—and that, in many ways, is the essence of life. It is what pushes us to bring value to life.

Yes, bad things do happen. Terrible things do. But we don't often count the good. We cringe over tragic traffic accidents, but don't consider the fact that all day long, by the millions, cars are zooming past each other at impossible speeds and within reaching distance—and nothing happens. We despise murders, but sometimes forget to note that billions of us live together each day and manage to work things out without violence.

**You cannot hold on to anything good. You must be continually giving—and getting.**

*Robert Collier*
*(American author, 1885–1950)*

What none of us can understand is why some people deliberately do terrible things to others. Evil, to me, isn't the work of the devil, but the work of the unknown. We are by nature animals—tribal, protective, suspicious—and we have to work very hard to understand why we sometimes act as we do and how we can prevent the unthinkable from happening more than it does. Your teacher who said it is better to light a candle than to curse the darkness said it all in very few words.

My own life was changed by an experience I had in the Far North. I had travelled there to do a magazine story about the Crees of James Bay, natives who were setting up the first self-government after reaching a settlement with the Canadian and Quebec governments over a vast hydroelectric development that required the flooding of several rivers. As part of the settlement, they were to get new housing, but the governments failed to finish off the promised homes and sewers. The wells became poisoned and several babies died from gastroenteritis, typically a Third World disease. I spent a great deal of time with the Crees, saw how they fought for their rights, and was able to write a story about their situation that caught the attention of the World Health Organization, which put an end to the poisoned water. I learned, at that moment, that it is possible to do something to help others, and there has never been a better feeling in my entire career than at the moment when the governments decided to move in and fix things. It was one small story, and the vast amount of work was done by the Crees themselves, but to be even a small part of such a profound experience changed my life and my approach to my work. You can indeed change the world.

One person can make a difference.

Two can make a bigger difference.

And the difference that would be possible if everyone tried a little harder is impossible to imagine.

Which, when you think about it, is exactly as it should be.

Sincerely,
Roy MacGregor

# DAVID MATAS

David Matas was born on August 29, 1943, in Winnipeg, Manitoba. He received a B.A. from the University of Manitoba, an M.A. from Princeton, and a B.A. (Jurisprudence) and Bachelor of Civil Law from Oxford University.

He has been extensively involved with many organizations, including Amnesty International, B'nai Brith, the Canadian Bar Association, the Canadian Council for Refugees, the Canadian Jewish Congress, and the International Commission for Jurists.

For his dedication to human rights, he has received numerous awards, academic appointments, and honours, including the Governor General's Confederation Medal, the B'nai Brith Presidential Citation, Vancouver Interfaith Brotherhood Person of the Year, International Commission of Jurists Walter Tarnopolsky Human Rights Award, and the Asia Pacific Human Rights Watch Charitable Trust Guardian of Justice Award.

David is the acclaimed author of sixteen books and manuscripts, the most recent being *Aftershock: Anti-Zionism and Anti-Semitism*, published by Dundurn Press in 2005.

He continues to travel throughout the

Disciplining yourself to do what you know is right and important, although difficult, is the highroad to pride, self-esteem, and personal satisfaction.

*Margaret Thatcher*
*(British prime minister, 1925–)*

world, lending his voice, reputation, and expertise to upholding human rights, observing trials and elections, and acting as a champion of the oppressed.

For more Information:
**www.amnesty.org**
**www.amnesty.ca**

David Matas

**Always do right. This will gratify some people and astonish the rest.**

**Mark Twain**
*(American author and humorist, 1835–1910)*

Dear Jo,

It is something that did *not* happen to me that made me want to help people. I was born in Winnipeg during the Holocaust, the Nazi killing of eleven million innocents—including six million Jews—and the attempt to kill all Jews worldwide. It did not take me long to realize that I was lucky to be alive.

Strictly speaking, I am not a survivor of the Holocaust, since all four of my grandparents came to Canada before the First World War. Yet, in a very real sense, I and every other Jewish person are survivors of the Holocaust. Six million Jews were killed. All Jews were targeted. It is only the fortunes of war that led to an Allied rather than an Axis victory in the Second World War. If the Axis powers had won, not one Jewish person would be alive today.

From the time that I was eight or nine, I remember being horrified by the Holocaust and wanting to do something about it. At eight or nine, I was not quite sure what that something would be. But as I grew older and became involved in human rights

> I think one's feelings waste themselves in words; they ought all to be distilled into actions which bring results.
>
> **Florence Nightingale**
> *(English nurse and war hero, 1820–1910)*

activities, it became clearer to me what that something was.

If we are to give any meaning at all to the meaningless slaughter of so many millions of innocents, we must learn the lessons of the Holocaust. I have been involved in human rights work in four different ways: refugee work, attempts to bring fugitive war criminals to justice, advocacy of the banning of hate speech, and challenges to a long list of human rights violations abroad. This involvement is the result of four conclusions that I have drawn about the Holocaust. The Holocaust would not have happened if, at that time, there had been an effective and universal system in place to bring mass murderers to justice; if refugees fleeing persecution had been offered protection; if laws had worked effectively to ban the propagation of hatred; and if people everywhere had protested gross violations of human rights as they occurred.

There is a tendency to turn to governments or to the United Nations to promote respect for human rights. Yet, human rights belong to individuals. Unless individuals, both adults

**The only thing necessary for the triumph of evil is for good men to do nothing.**

*Edmund Burke*
*(Irish philosopher, 1729–1797)*

and children, promote respect for human rights, these rights are bound to wither.

There is nothing that we, children or adults, can do now to save those already killed in massive human rights tragedies. But, if they are not to have died in vain, we must prevent such tragedies from ever happening again. We must learn the lessons that our predecessors ignored. To me, those lessons are: bring mass murderers to justice; ban hate speech; protect refugees; and never accept in silence gross violations of human rights, wherever they may occur. But, the ultimate point I want to make is not so much the need to learn these four lessons as it is the need to draw our own lessons from human rights tragedies.

There is a natural tendency for us to avert our eyes from any horror. But these are monsters we must stare in the face.

The lessons to be learned from flagrant human rights violations are ones we must learn ourselves. They will not descend from heaven like the holy texts. Rather, they ascend from hell, from the inferno of human rights tragedies. We cannot expect one child to erase

> It has become appallingly obvious that our technology has exceeded our humanity.
>
> *Albert Einstein*
> *(German scientist, 1879–1955)*

all of society's evil, but the innocence of a child should become society's conscience.

When a person suffers from human rights violations, often the worst of it is not so much the physical suffering as it is the demoralization. Global solidarity, support from outsiders, awareness that the victim is not alone, and recognition that what has been done to the victim is wrong counter this demoralization and combat the victimization.

While, for victims, support from anywhere is welcome, nothing matches the voice of a child. Poet William Wordsworth wrote, "The Child is father of the Man." The human rights violations about which I became aware as a child, the atrocities of the Holocaust, are the ones burned most deeply into my soul. So it is with any child.

The voice of a child tells the victim that not only do we know and care about their victimization now, we will know and care about it in the future. The voice of a child is the voice of the next generation. The voice of a child protesting human rights violations is a statement that the future people of the

**To ignore evil is to become an accomplice to it.**

*Martin Luther King, Jr.*
*(American activist, visionary, and minister, 1929–1968)*

world will know and care about what was done to the victim. And that, for the victim, is a special form of redress.

I hope this helps.

Best regards,
David Matas

> Ideas must work through the brains and the arms of good and brave men, or they are no better than dreams.
>
> **Ralph Waldo Emerson**
> *(American poet and philosopher, 1803–1882)*

# ROBERT MUNSCH

Robert Munsch was born on June 11, 1945, in Pittsburgh, Pennsylvania, one of nine children. He reports that school was a challenge, but he always wrote poetry—something that most people didn't think had much value. He received a B.A. in history and a master's in anthropology and studied for seven years to become a Jesuit priest. While studying for this career, he worked part-time at an orphanage and discovered the joy of working with children. He ultimately decided against the priesthood and began working in a daycare centre, discovering that this was in fact the career he wished to pursue. He attended the Elliot Pearson School of Child Studies at Tufts University and, while on placement, wrote his first story—which eleven years later became *Mortimer.* He and his wife emigrated to Canada and began working at the lab preschool at Guelph University.

Robert was always telling stories to the children, but never writing them down. Finally, taking time off work to write, he completed his first story, *Mud Puddle.* It was rejected by nine publishers and accepted by the tenth. He went on to write forty-two books, speak to hundreds of thousands of children and adults, and become

**If you want to lift yourself up, lift up someone else.**

*Booker T. Washington*
*(American educator, 1856–1915)*

Canada's all-time bestselling writer with more than thirty million copies sold. He has been awarded Author of the Year by the Canadian Booksellers Association, has received the Vicky Metcalf Award for a body of work, and was named to the Order of Canada.

Robert is now a Canadian citizen and he and his wife reside in Guelph, Ontario.

The task of the educator lies in seeing that the child does not confound good with immobility and evil with activity.

*Maria Montessori*
*(Italian physician and educational pioneer, 1870–1952)*

Robert Munsch

Hi Jo,

Once I was walking home late at night and all of a sudden I found myself crawling and wondering why the sidewalk was so full of blood. Some nutcase had tried to kill me with a baseball bat, and had left me for dead. It was an honest mistake, because I really looked dead and I had amnesia and a lot of my brain stuff never worked very well after that. Some things you just can't plan for. Bad things just happen sometimes. It doesn't make them right. They just happen.

Check out this remembered bit of news:

October 7, 1969—CBC

Montreal is in a state of shock. A police officer is dead and 108 people have been arrested following 16 hours of chaos during which police and firefighters refused to work. At first, the strike's impact was limited to more bank robberies than normal. But as night fell, a taxi drivers' union seized upon the police absence to violently protest a competitor's exclusive right to airport pickups. The result, according to this CBC

**It's not enough that we do our best; sometimes we have to do what's required.**

*Winston Churchill*
*(British prime minister and orator, 1874–1965)*

Television special, was a "night of terror." Shattered shop windows and a trail of broken glass are evidence of looting that erupted in the downtown core. With no one to stop them, students and separatists joined the rampage. Shop owners, some of them armed, struggled to fend off looters. Restaurants and hotels were also targeted. A corporal with the Quebec provincial police was shot and killed at the garage of the Murray Hill limousine company as taxi drivers tried to burn it down.

As police returned to duty in the wee hours, the arrests began. By morning, the city's public buildings were under guard by the army, which was summoned by Premier Jean-Jacques Bertrand. At least twenty people have been injured, and damage from the riot has been estimated at $2 million ($10.7 million in 2005 dollars).

Now, that is in nice, "peaceful" Canada. No Cops = Major Mess!

A man from Lebanon once said to me: "It is nice you have an army here. In Lebanon we

> **There is no failure except in no longer trying.**
>
> *Elbert Hubbard*
> *(American author,*
> *1956–1915)*

did not have a real central government army and soon each little group had its *own* army and then all the groups started fighting and everything fell apart."

So, how people act depends on the society they live in and on the reasons that society gives them to follow a rule of law. In lawless situations, people are really nasty. Keeping a society just (so that people think things are fair) and fed and educated and clothed is never a simple thing that happens automatically. Society is more like a plant than a machine that does not change. If we let Canada get too far off track, all hell will break loose here just as it did in Somalia or the Sudan. So, look at your own town and country and try to keep it running well!

At the international level, most countries act only out of self-interest. The Rich World that makes stuff does not care about the Poor World that grows stuff. Look at international trade, see how it is not fair, and try to change it. A lot of countries are quite small in terms of power when compared to big companies, so these countries can be funded by companies rather than by taxpayers, and then their

**You cannot shake hands with a clenched fist.**

*Indira Gandhi*
*(Indian politician, 1917–1984)*

governments can do whatever they want. A good society balances the needs of individuals, groups, and corporations. This is a real balancing act that changes with time.

Anyway, try to change the *system*, because that leads to real, long-term change. Most of the wars going on today are systemic wars. They would not be happening if there was a different system of international trade and law.

> Good works are links that form a chain of love.
>
> ***Mother Teresa***
> *(Catholic nun, missionary, and humanitarian, 1910–1997)*

But remember!

1.  Things may not be as bad as you think. News rarely covers good things.
2.  The world is not small. It is really big and people around the world think really differently and experience it really differently. There are *no* simple solutions.
3.  Pick one thing to work on, learn about it, and then figure out what you can do.

Bye,
Robert

# PAUL NALLANAYAGAM

Paul Nallanayagam was born in Jaffna, Ceylon (now known as Sri Lanka), on February 23, 1925. He graduated with a B.A. in economics from the University of Ceylon in 1948. He married Bertha Swarnam and they had three daughters, Nirmala, Koshala, and Vathsala. His family emigrated to Canada in 1972. In 1979, he returned to Sri Lanka, where he and his wife ran the Methodist Girls' Home, an orphanage in Kalmunai.

In 1985, Paul was jailed for 122 days on Slave Island, held in a small cell, sleeping on a concrete floor, the last half of that time spent in solitary confinement. Despite the threat of life in prison, he refused to compromise his principles or to deny the truth. He credits the work of Amnesty International as a primary reason for his ultimate release.

Paul now lives in Toronto to be close to members of his family. His wife died in 2006. He remains a man willing to speak out against injustice.

For more information: **www.amnesty.ca**

> **You get from the world what you give to the world.**
>
> *Oprah Winfrey*
> *(American broadcaster and humanitarian, 1954–)*

Hello Jo,

I was born in a country called Sri Lanka, which is a large island at the southern tip of India. Sri Lanka is considered by many people to be one of the most beautiful places on earth. Sadly, for the past four decades it has also been one of the most unhappy places on earth because of a civil war between its two largest ethnic groups.

My family emigrated to Canada in the 1970s so that my three daughters could grow up in a safe country. In 1982, with my daughters well established in Canada, my wife and I decided to return to Sri Lanka to run an orphanage for the Methodist church in Kalmunai, a town in the eastern part of the island. Although fighting raged all around us, we worked for peace. I even became president of the local Citizens Committee for National Harmony, an organization that attempted to help victims of the fighting.

In July 1983, some local people came to our orphanage to report that the Sri Lankan military had arrested twenty-three young Tamil men from a nearby village. They asked if I could find out what had happened to their children. I phoned the local military camps and police stations but did not get any satisfactory answers. Several days later, I heard a horrible rumour that the bodies of these twenty-three teenagers, along with thirty-six others, had been found buried in a mass grave. I went to the site myself, saw a great deal of blood on the ground, and found an identity card belonging to one of the missing boys.

By the time I returned to the orphanage, news of the massacre was beginning to leak to the outside world. Foreign reporters in Colombo, Sri Lanka's capital, called me to ask about the killings and I told them what I had seen. A few days later, a van carrying four policemen arrived at the orphanage. They said that their commanding officer wanted me to come to the station to make an official statement. I climbed into the van fully expecting to be back for dinner. Instead, I was thrown in jail!

To avoid the humiliation of having to let me go, I was officially charged with spreading false rumours about the Sri Lankan military,

**He who does a good deed will have ten times the amount of blessings.**

*Muhammad*
*(Prophet and founder of Islam, 570–632)*

spreading lies to the public, and giving false information to the foreign media. The Sri Lankan government transferred me to a new jail with the ominous name of Slave Island in Colombo, Sri Lanka's capital. The cells were like cages in a very bad zoo. Each was about twelve feet square with about twenty prisoners crammed inside. There was no place to sleep except on the concrete floor, and this was very hard to do because each cell was so crowded. Many of the other prisoners were dangerous criminals. The police kept me in jail for weeks without charging me. Because this is illegal, my wife, Swarnam, and the Citizens Committee for National Harmony hired lawyers to demand my release.

These were very serious charges. If convicted, I could expect to spend the rest of my life in jail. To add to our woes, my wife and I had already spent nearly every cent we had on lawyers' fees. With no more money for lawyers, I knew I almost certainly would be convicted of the false charges.

The Sri Lankan government knew there was little truth to the charges, so they offered me a deal. If I would publicly declare that I had lied about the massacre, they would drop the charges and my wife and I would be allowed to leave the country.

I thought long and hard about my choices. If convicted, my wife would live the rest of her life without me. My daughters would likely never see me again. I thought about those tiny cells crammed with dangerous criminals and how horrible it would be to spend the rest of my life there.

Jo, faced with all of these horrible things, I admit I was very tempted to give in. All I had to do was tell a lie and I would be a free man. But then I thought about the many families who had lost their loved ones in the massacre. If I accepted the government's offer, there would never be justice for those fifty-nine boys and the killers would be allowed to go on performing their terrible work. With my heart trembling, I said no and the government officers went away very angry.

They say that good things come in threes, and that is what happened soon after I turned down the deal. First, my wife had contacted the Canadian embassy and they informed the Sri Lankan government that they were monitoring my case closely. Second, Amnesty International began reporting on my trial to the world. Third, Somasunderam Nadesan, one of the greatest lawyers in Sri Lanka, came out of retirement to represent me—for free!

**Do not be overcome by evil, but overcome evil with good.**

*Romans 12:21*

With the Canadian government and Amnesty International focusing the eyes of the world on Sri Lanka, I was moved to a private cell where I was much safer. Because the government case was a web of lies, Mr. Nadesan had no trouble making the government officers look like fools in court. After a forty-nine-day trial, I was found innocent of all charges and set free.

My wife and I moved back to Canada as soon as possible. Although I am happy to be reunited with my entire family again, I can never forget the fact that the killers of those fifty-nine boys were never brought to justice. The war continues to rage, and innocent people are killed on both sides nearly every day. I believe that the only way to stop the war is for more world attention to be brought to what the government is doing in Sri Lanka.

Even the most powerful governments are afraid of bad publicity. Amnesty International and PEN are two organizations who have saved many lives just by writing letters that exposed what bad governments were up to. You can do the same. Write to Members of Parliament and ask them what Canada is doing about situations around the world where you see injustices being done. You'll be amazed at the difference you can make.

Paul

Paul Nallanayagam

# Injustice anywhere is a threat to justice everywhere.

**Martin Luther King, Jr.**
*(American activist, visionary, and minister, 1929–1968)*

# KIM PHUC

Kim Phuc was born and raised in Trang Bang, a small community north of Saigon, during the Vietnam War. In 1972, at the age of nine, while fleeing for safety, she and others were mistakenly bombed with napalm by a South Vietnamese airplane. More than half of her body suffered third-degree burns and she was not expected to live. She was hospitalized for fourteen months, had seventeen surgical procedures, and lived through extensive and painful therapy that allowed her to live and leave the hospital.

The tragedy of her near death was captured by Associated Press photographer Nick Ut. The picture was a defining moment in the Vietnam War, won the Pulitzer Prize, and became a visual representation of the horror of the war and its effects on the most innocent victims: children.

Kim remained in Vietnam after the country fell to communism. As an adult, she and her husband defected in 1992, taking refuge in Canada. In 1994, she became a Goodwill Ambassador for UNESCO, travelling the world to speak out about the terrible effects of war on children and the need for peace, love, and forgiveness.

**A people that values its privileges above its principles soon loses both.**

*Dwight D. Eisenhower*
*(American president, 1890–1969)*

She founded the Kim Foundation, whose mission is "to help heal the wounds suffered by innocent children and to restore hope and happiness to their lives, by providing much-needed medical and psychological assistance." It funds projects around the world to carry out this mission.

Kim resides in Ajax, Ontario, with her husband and two children, Thomas and Stephen.

For more information:
**www.kimfoundation.com**

**We are rich only through what we give, and poor only through what we refuse.**

*Ann-Sophie Swetchine*
*(writer, 1782–1857)*

ANNE BAYIN

Kim Phuc

Dear Jo,

I grew up in a little village called Trang Bang in Vietnam. It was about twenty-five miles northeast of Saigon on the highway that led to Non Phen. It wasn't a large village, maybe five hundred people, but it was my home. I lived with my parents and eight brothers and sisters, but all around me were my relatives. There was no place I could go where I didn't know the people and where I wasn't cared for. This was a wonderful place to grow up.

Unfortunately, my country was involved in a war—one that had been going on for longer than I had been alive. While our village was considered pretty safe, we saw evidence of the war all the time. Other people, people no different than you or me, were forced from their homes by the bombs and guns and fighting. Many of them came to our village. They didn't have food or a place to live, but we welcomed them and helped them. My grandparents and my parents offered them places to build huts and shared what food we had. That was the way my parents were. They were kind to their children and relatives, but also to people they didn't know.

> **Forgiveness is a virtue of the brave.**
>
> *Indira Gandhi*
> *(Indian politician, 1917–1984)*

The war that had been raging throughout the country got bigger and closer to home. We had to flee our village and we took refuge in the Cao Dai Temple. But we weren't safe. The air force, thinking they were attacking the enemy, dropped napalm. Napalm is a type of bomb filled with different chemicals, including gasoline, that causes everything it touches to break into flame. Napalm fell all over me. I don't remember all of what happened next—although I was told about it all later— but more than 65 percent of my body was burned. What I do remember is the pain. Not just the pain of my body being burned but of the months and months of rehabilitation I spent trying to regain the use of my body, to try to overcome what had been done to me.

The doctors didn't think I would live. I lived. They didn't think I could recover. I recovered. Both of these things were nothing short of a miracle. I thank God for that.

I was blessed to be part of a large, caring family. I saw the best of people. I also saw war and the very worst of what people can do to each other. I have spent a great deal of my

> **The example of great and pure characters is the only thing that can produce fine ideas and noble deeds.**
>
> **Albert Einstein**
> *(German scientist, 1879–1955)*

life's journey trying to understand how people can be capable of such acts of kindness and cruelty. I have come to realize that there is only one thing that separates those who do good from those who do evil. That one thing is love. Love for each other.

Rather than hate, we must understand that we are the same. We cannot be greedy; we cannot hate. We must forgive and show true love for each other. This is something that we are all capable of doing.

> The true measure of a man is how he treats someone who can do him absolutely no good.
>
> **Samuel Johnson**
> *(English writer, 1709–1784)*

What happened to me—and I still bear the scars and feel the physical pain daily—could have made me angry and bitter. It could have made me hate those that hurt me, or hate other people. I hate no one. I have learned to forgive and to love. I understand that none of us are perfect humans, but we are perfectly human—we make mistakes, we learn, we grow. I have learned that through true love I can forgive and be happy.

As I said, it was a miracle that I lived. Perhaps it was an even greater miracle that I discovered forgiveness and love. Now, it is my obligation to help other people to understand that the cure for hate is love, to understand that we are all the same, that we are just humans. I speak out for those who have no voices, the victims of violence, hoping that my words will help others to discover the course of forgiveness. I will continue to offer my words, my experiences, and my hope for the rest of my life.

You are young. You wonder if a child—one child—can do anything to make the world a better place. This is such an important question. And the answer is simple. The world can only become a better place one person at a time—one child at a time. Each day, you should work to love others, help others, and forgive others. This starts with your family. Listen to your parents, love your brothers and sisters, love your aunts and uncles. Then remember that we are all part of the same big family. No matter what people look like on the outside, we are all the same on the inside. We are one big family. Help the rest of your family wherever you can and the world will become a better place.

Mother Teresa said that perhaps we are not capable of great things, but that each of us is

## The best politics is right action.

**Mahatma Gandhi**
*(Indian politician, activist, and visionary, 1869–1948)*

capable of doing small things with great love. One by one, these small acts will make a difference. By asking these questions, Jo, I know that you are somebody who wants to make a difference. I am proud of you.

With love,
Kim Phuc

The good man is the friend of all living things.

*Mahatma Gandhi*
*(Indian politician, activist,*
*and visionary, 1869–1948)*

# JOHNNIE AND JEROME WILLIAMS

Johnnie (March 15, 1972) and Jerome (May 10, 1973) Williams were born in Washington, D.C. Given the support, encouragement, and direction of their family, the two boys developed a commitment to learning and a love of sports, eventually becoming aspiring basketball stars. Johnnie's dream to play ball ended in his senior year of high school when his elbow was shattered during a game. Jerome went on to play at Georgetown College, where he earned a B.Sc. in sociology and the Raymond Medley Student Athlete Award. Jerome began his NBA career with the Detroit Pistons, eventually playing 587 games in 9 seasons with 4 teams. In each team's city, along with brother Johnnie, he launched programs to increase literacy and to inspire, motivate, and encourage young people. For these efforts, Jerome received the Fannie Mae Foundation's 2000 Home Team Community Service Award.

Johnnie has become a youth activist and motivational speaker who travels nationally and internationally, connecting with audiences around the world. After retiring from basketball, Jerome became a Community Ambassador for

**I would like to be known as a person who is concerned about freedom and equality and justice and prosperity for all people.**

*Rosa Parks*
*(American civil rights pioneer, 1913–2005)*

the NBA Basketball Without Borders program, travelling to Asia and Africa to help promote fair play, teamwork, and the life principles found in basketball while bringing resources to these areas of the world.

The two brothers remain committed to trying to make a difference in the world.

For more information: **www.bookjohnnie.com**

**Knowing that for whatever good anyone does, he will receive his reward from the Lord.**

*Ephesians 6:8*

Johnnie and Jerome WIlliams

Dear Jo,

Can you imagine being on a basketball court, playing on an NBA team, with twenty thousand screaming fans in the stands and hundreds of thousands more watching at home on their televisions, and getting paid millions to play the game you love?

For many people that would be a dream come true. For my brother, Jerome, that was not just a dream, but a reality, the life he was leading. And while he loved his life and loved the game he always knew that there was more to life, more that he *could* do and *should* do. What a person does on the court makes them a good player. What they do once they step off the court can make them a good person.

Jerome and I were blessed to grow up in a strong family. We have two parents who not only showed us love, acceptance and caring, but also provided us with guidance, direction, and strength. There was no question that our parents loved us, but also no question that they demanded that we do our best. And while we had that foundation,

> **A life has no value except in the impact it has on others.**
>
> *Jackie Robinson*
> *(American baseball player and integration pioneer, 1919–1972)*

unfortunately many people do not. We want to reach out and help people and teach youth around the world the values we were given by our parents.

Jerome knew that being a member of the NBA was not just a privilege, but a way to open doors. Together, he and I decided we wanted to do more. We wanted to be more than just a part of the world, we wanted to *Change the World*. We started by going into the communities, working with young people, first in Detroit, then Toronto, Chicago and New York. We traveled, speaking to youth groups, schools, church communities, trying to provide inspiration, encouragement, leadership, and began to create and fund programs to promote literacy, life skills and leadership, helping boys and girls become responsible men and women. Through these efforts we have reached out to more than one million youth. We have made a choice to give something back. We have chosen not to waste time, nor the opportunity to change the world in our unique way. Time waits no man; you can only waste it or maximize it. Always remember that!

> Love cannot remain by itself—it has no meaning. Love has to be put into action, and that action is service.
>
> **Mother Teresa**
> *(Catholic nun, missionary, and humanitarian, 1910–1997)*

Professional sports figures can certainly be people you can look up to. That doesn't necessarily make them heroes. Think about the people who help you learn new skills or ideas, put food on the table for you, support you when you're sad, help you back to your feet when you fall, encourage you, take care of you when you're sick. Those are the people— parents, grandparents, aunts and uncles, older siblings, teachers, coaches and mentors—who are the real heroes. Always remember that!

Jerome retired from playing in the NBA three years early, leaving offers to continue playing for millions of dollars on the table. That choice allows us to focus on the big picture: the world picture. It shocked so many people that a popular ball player would just walk away, but they didn't understand that we have a much bigger assignment that awaits us. I believe that you already know what it is.

As I write this letter we are in Shaghai, China. We have been part of helping to get out a global message on HIV/AIDS awareness, empowerment, and to help young people understand that they have a choice to make to improve their lives and in turn the lives of those around them.

So many people minimize their potential impact on the world by retaining the mindset, "who am I to think I could change the world, I'm only one person?" To them we ask the following question–

What happens when you throw a huge rock in a pond? Now what happens when you throw a small pebble into the same pond? The water responds to both, just as the world will respond to any and all gestures of goodwill and humanity of any size or type. Always remember that!

That's one of the things that we were taught growing up. It's something we want to pass on. We try to teach that power is in the choice not the action; actions create circumstances that result from a good or bad choice. So many people have felt devalued for most of their lives, causing them to give up on themselves, thus giving up on humanity. Think of how much has been lost, not just for them, but for the good they could have done for others.

> Darkness cannot drive out darkness; only light can do that. Hate cannot drive out hate; only love can do that.
>
> *Martin Luther King*
> *(American activist,*
> *visionary, and minister,*
> *1929–1968)*

Jo, your letter has let me know that you haven't given up. Your questions have caused ripples in the pond of life and you may never know or see the shores your waves may wash upon, but know that someone, somewhere appreciates you and your efforts to change the world.

Always remember that our efforts + your efforts + others' efforts = World Change.

Johnnie and Jerome 'Junkyard Dog' Williams

# ETHAN ZOHN

Ethan was born in 1973 in Lexington, Massachusetts. He graduated from Vassar College in upstate New York, going on to play professional soccer for Highlanders FC (Zimbabwe), Cape Cod Crusaders (Massachusetts, USA) and Hawaii Tsunami (Hawaii, USA). Ethan also played for the 1997 and 2001 U.S. Maccabiah squads.

After winning *Survivor Africa* in 2002, Ethan co-founded Grassroot Soccer (**www.grassrootsoccer.org**), a nonprofit organization that trains professional soccer players to teach African children, through a tailor-made curriculum, about HIV/AIDS prevention. Since its founding GRS has "graduated" over 230,000 youths. By the FIFA World Cup in South Africa in 2010, the organization's goal is to graduate one million African youths from the program.

In 2008, Ethan launched Grassroot Soccer UNITED (**www.grassrootsoccer.org**), an international, youth-led movement to raise money and build awareness for his foundation and mission to end HIV/AIDS in Africa.

Ethan is also the national spokesperson for America Scores, an organization that helps inner-city kids participate in educational soccer programs. Other extensive charity work includes the Elizabeth Glazer Pediatric AIDS Foundation, KickAIDS, the Colon Cancer Alliance and Autism Speaks.

In recognition for his charitable work Ethan has been awarded the Nkosi Johnson Community Spirit Award by the International Association of Physicians in AIDS Care, the Heroes Among Us Award from the Boston Celtics and the Massachusetts State Health Department, and the Auxilia Chimusoro Award from the U.S. State Department in Zimbabwe.

**Ethan Zohn**

Hello Jo,

I was lucky to be chosen out of 60,000 applicants to be part of *Survivor Africa*. There I was on a famous television show, watched by millions of people, and through a combination of skill, strategy, hard work and athleticism I was the last survivor. I'd won. I had riches, a bit of fame and opportunities to live the jet-set lifestyle. But that wasn't what I wanted.

*Survivor Africa* took place in Kenya. I was greatly affected by my time there—inspired by the beauty of the land and the spirit of the people. I was also deeply impacted by witnessing the tragedies of the HIV/AIDS pandemic first hand. Africa had become a part of my life and I couldn't simply walk away from the devastation there because it was too big or too overwhelming for one person. What could I possibly do to affect a change?

The answer was right in front of me. I have always played, and loved soccer, and knew that the game was deeply ingrained in African culture. I invested the money that I had won, along with my new more public

> **Do not wait for leaders; do it alone, person to person.**
>
> **Mother Teresa**
> *(Catholic nun, missionary, and humanitarian, 1910–1997)*

profile, to co-found Grassroot Soccer. Our team's mission is to mobilize the global soccer community to combat the AIDS epidemic in Africa. By utilizing the popularity of the game we provide African youth with the knowledge, skills and support to live HIV free.

There are many reasons why I felt I needed to do more, but the most important are the things that happened to me in my life when I was much younger.

Loss, heartbreak, pain, death. These seemed very remote and distant to me as a fourteen-year-old boy. These were concepts that I had read about in books, seen in movies, or that had happened to a friend of a friend. Suddenly these were no longer concepts. They had changed my life forever.

In the fifteen years since my father died of colorectal cancer I have learned much about life. I have learned to separate the important from the trivial. I have learned what to throw away and what to keep. I can appreciate the precious nature of time and the passion that any part of a minute can bring.

I have learned that to make happiness real for others is the greatest gift. It provides the foundation for celebration of life. My dad taught me this. I honor him by living each day fully and joyously, striving for hard to reach goals. I treasure this legacy.

I have seen the results. We have empowered youth across Africa. It means so much to me when a twelve-year-old boy, in Bulawayo, Zimbabwe, who had graduated from Grassroots Soccer, tells me that "Doctors and Scientist are trying their best, but the duty is in our hands, we can make a difference—now let's go out there!"

I believe that we all can make a difference—young or old. You've asked questions that show you want to help and I believe that you can be one of those people. If you want to know the definition of fulfillment, I say follow your heart, fight for a cause, see the hope that is born in someone else's eyes because of something you were able to do for them.

Ethan

PART 2

# BILAAL
# RAJAN

# PROBLEM, WHAT PROBLEM?

Bilaal Rajan doesn't see problems. It isn't that he doesn't see things that are wrong, things that need to be fixed or corrected. He just doesn't see problems. He only sees solutions.

From a very young age, Bilaal was aware of the world around him. Not just his home, where he lives with his parents and dog, Bobbi, or his Toronto neighbourhood, but the world.

In 2001, when Bilaal was just four years old, he heard about a terrible tragedy in India. An earthquake had hit that part of the world and thousands had been injured, killed, and left homeless. Watching scenes of the devastation on television, Bilaal didn't really know where India was, but he did know that people needed help. With the assistance of his parents, he began to go door to door, selling clementine oranges. Working persistently—because persistence is one of Bilaal's strongest traits—he eventually sold enough oranges to raise $350. This was his first attempt to help others, but his parents knew right then that it wouldn't be his last.

Bilaal educated himself about issues surrounding global poverty. He learned that while he and his family lived a comfortable life, there were people—children— around the world who had very little. Taking part in the

## It isn't enough to talk about peace. One must believe in it. And it isn't enough to believe in it. One must work at it.

*Eleanor Roosevelt*
*(American social activist and wife of President Franklin D. Roosevelt,*
*1884–1962)*

World Partnership Walk (www.worldpartnershipwalk.com) from 2000 to 2004, Bilaal raised more than $1000 in support of global poverty.

In September 2004, a hurricane caused devastation on the small island nation of Haiti. Once again, Bilaal saw a situation that needed his assistance. He asked if his father's company could donate boxes of cookies that he could sell to raise funds. In addition to selling cookies personally door to door, at his school, and at public gatherings, Bilaal recruited a team of twelve children to help him. Within one month, they were able to present a cheque for $6387 to UNICEF for Haiti disaster aid.

Subsequently, Bilaal began to make and sell decorative acrylic plates. This raised an additional $1200. Despite these incredible efforts to raise funds and help others, Bilaal was only beginning his humanitarian work.

On December 26, 2004, the entire world watched in horror as a tsunami swept through Southeast Asia, killing tens of thousands and displacing millions. We all bore witness to perhaps the greatest natural tragedy of our generation. Once again, Bilaal knew he had work to do.

In his role as UNICEF spokeschild, he issued the Canada Kids Earthquake Challenge (www.unicef.ca). Bilaal personally made a commitment to raise $10,000 and

> To be good, we must do good; and by doing good we take a sure means of being good, as the use and exercise of the muscles increase their power.

**Tryon Edwards**
*(American theologian and writer, 1809–1894)*

challenged children across the country to help raise funds as well. Ultimately, Bilaal raised more than $50,000, and his challenge resulted in more than $5 million in aid.

Not satisfied with simply raising funds, Bilaal convinced his parents to take him to the places where the tsunami had caused the most destruction. They travelled to Indonesia, Sri Lanka, Thailand, and the Maldives, where they could not only witness the destruction, but also see the efforts to rebuild, and be able to report these efforts to the Canadian children who had raised funds. With his typical straightforward approach, Bilaal asked the president of the Maldives why the rebuilding wasn't going more

# Happiness is not a goal; it is a by-product.

*Eleanor Roosevelt*
*(American social activist and wife of Franklin D. Roosevelt, 1884–1962)*

quickly. He needed to know that every effort was being made to get help to those who needed it so desperately.

Impressed with Bilaal's efforts, UNICEF Canada named him their official spokeschild in Canada in February 2005. He quickly proved their wisdom by, among other initiatives, approaching major corporations for donations to further aid Haiti. A major drug company provided prescription medication while a food company donated two thousand cases of baby food.

Balaal is also the author of *Making Change: Tips from an Underage Overachiever*. He has recently established a prize at his school to recognize the middle school student who devotes the most hours to a volunteer cause.

Despite all of his accomplishments—which seem almost superhuman—Bilaal is just a very nice, normal, twelve-year-old boy. He loves to spend time with his dog, Bobby; play sports such as soccer, lacrosse, swimming, and tennis; build robots with Lego bricks; talk to his friends; and play on his keyboard.

His parents know that Bilaal is, by nature, very energetic. He has bursts of creativity, moves around the room, taps his fingers while he talks, and is constantly in motion. His mother, Shamim, readily admits that keeping up with him can be exhausting at times, but she and her husband

A kind man who makes good use of wealth is rightly said to possess a great treasure; but the miser who hoards up his riches will have no profit.

*Buddha*
*(Founder of Buddhism, 560 BC –486 BC)*

work hard to nurture Bilaal's interests and to support him in his worthy projects. Bilaal is fascinated by the world around him and immerses himself in new ideas. There is no telling where Bilaal will next another solution. What is certain is that it will happen again . . . and again . . . and again. Equally certain is that his parents will be there beside him, guiding and supporting while allowing him to explore these new avenues.

For more information about Bilaal's projects have a look at www.handsforhelp.org and www.makingchange now.com.

# HANNAH

# TAYLOR

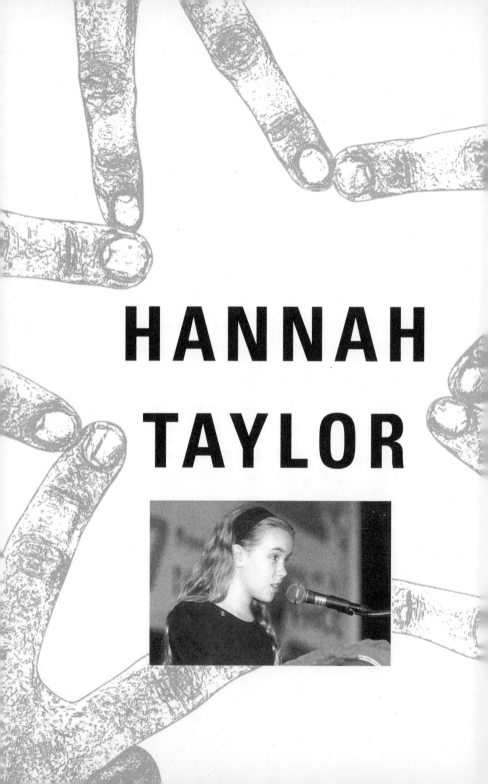

# I WISH I COULD
# CURE HOMELESSNESS

At age 5, Hannah Taylor was driving home with her mother, safely cocooned within the family car, protected from the winter weather of Winnipeg. She was singing "Jingle Bells." Hannah loves to sing. As the car came to a stop at an intersection, she saw something right outside the window, only a few feet from her. A man was eating from a garbage can. Hannah watched in disbelief, unable to understand what he was doing. In the few seconds before they drove away, Hannah pointed out the man to her mother and asked her for an explanation. Her mother mumbled a few words, trying to explain that the man had nothing else to eat so he probably had no choice.

Many children wouldn't have noticed this man. Some would have noticed and not said anything. A few more would have been satisfied with the answer they were given and then gone back to singing, perhaps filling their minds with more pleasant thoughts—thoughts of dancing, or horseback riding, or school, or Christmas. But not Hannah.

When she got home, she asked her mother and then her father for a better explanation. Their attempts to explain the situation only created more questions. Not only had that man been eating from a garbage can, but he probably didn't have a home to go to, a place to sleep, or people who cared for him. Hannah continued to press for answers, asking her grandparents as well, but nobody seemed to be able to provide an explanation that could satisfy her. But then, what could an adequate explanation be? In a city with so much, in a country with so much, how could a person be relegated to eating from a garbage can and sleeping on the streets?

Hannah, the third of four children, was raised in a home filled with material comforts. But more important, it was filled with support and caring and love. Yet, from this place of plenty, her needs met and her interests encouraged, Hannah continued to think about that man and the others she occasionally saw wandering the streets of Winnipeg.

When I despair, I remember that all through history the ways of truth and love have always won. There have been tyrants, and murderers, and for a time they can seem invincible, but in the end they always fall. Think of it—always.

*Mahatma Gandhi*
*(Indian politician, activist, and visionary, 1869–1948)*

One of these was a woman who often appeared by Hannah's school. She was always bundled up against the weather and wind, and she pushed along a grocery cart piled with her possessions. This woman wasn't just a brief encounter through a car window, seen once and then gone. Instead, she was often there, waiting or walking, as Hannah was brought to and from school. Hannah knew she wanted to do something. Eventually, she asked her mother to stop the car and give the woman some change. This happened not once, not twice, but became such a pattern that her parents made sure they always had change or some food in the car to offer to the woman.

**We make a living by what we get,
but we make a life by what we give.**

*Winston Churchill*
*(British prime minister and orator, 1874–1965)*

The more contact Hannah had with the woman— the more she tried to do—the more she wanted to help and the more questions she had. One night, before going to bed, thinking about the homeless, Hannah talked to her mother about feeling sad and worried. Her mother told her that sometimes when you do something to change the problem, your heart isn't so sad. For Hannah, those few words went to both her heart and her head. She started thinking of ways to make a difference.

One of the first things she did was set up a meeting with her teacher, Mrs. Hildebrand, and her principal, Mrs. Steek. Over lunch, Hannah told them about the homeless and their needs, and about her desire to try to do something for them. She enlisted the help of her entire class and they decided to run a bake and art sale.

At this same time, her father made inquires, trying to arrange for Hannah to speak to somebody, perhaps visit a homeless shelter. He made contact with the executive director of the Siloam Mission, John Mohan, and a visit was arranged. Mr. Mohan said that he knew there was something different about Hannah right away. She wasn't there simply to observe but to interact. She talked to the men, asked them questions, gave them smiles and hugs. She didn't see them as homeless, but rather as *people* who were

**Anyone who prepares to do good must not expect people to roll stones out of his way, but must accept his lot calmly, even if they roll a few more upon it.**

*Albert Schweitzer*
*(German doctor and humanitarian, 1875–1965)*

homeless—people who needed to be talked to, cared for, and loved, in the same way that all people need those things as much as or more than they need food and shelter.

Mr. Mohan had shared his world with Hannah, so she asked if he would come and see part of her world, come to her school to talk to the students about the homeless. At the school he found not just a warm and receptive group of young people, but a group who had worked hard to raise money for the homeless. Their efforts resulted in the purchase of warm clothes, blankets, and hundreds of cans of coffee to help the people who used the mission.

Hannah had done something to help the homeless.

Something remarkable. Her parents were proud of her, but they thought—and secretly hoped—that perhaps this would now be enough and she could move on to pursue the interests of a typical six-year-old girl. Little did they realize that this wasn't the end, but only the beginning.

Looking around, Hannah was aware that so many people had so much and that they wouldn't have to give much to make a difference. She decided that to effect change, all she needed was a little bit of change—a few coins from people.

Hannah, with her mother's help, started decorating empty baby food jars to look like ladybugs. She'd always liked bugs—especially ladybugs, because they represent good luck and she felt that the people she was trying to help needed some luck. Eventually, she decorated three hundred Ladybug Jars and distributed them to local businesses and schools. A few pennies, nickels, a couple of dimes or quarters, and even dollars started to fill the jars. It was small change from thousands of people, but that small change created a big change—buying things for the homeless and helping to create perhaps the most important thing: hope.

Hannah was never content just to raise funds. Accompanied by one of her parents, she started to spend time at the missions and shelters that benefited from her

# To fail to do good is as bad as doing harm.

**Plutarch**
*(Greek philosopher, 45–125)*

fundraising efforts. She got to know the people and offered her hand and her hugs and her hope, letting them know that somebody cared.

Hannah also developed another goal: she didn't just want to raise funds, she wanted to raise awareness. She began speaking, first to students at her school, then at other schools, then to business leaders and politicians. She was interviewed on radio and television and for newspapers. Always, she spoke from the heart, talking about the facts and figures, the realities of homelessness, but also talking about the people behind those facts, the people she had come to know. She brought this message to some of the

> **What we have done for ourselves alone dies with us. What we have done for others and the world remains and is immortal.**
>
> *Albert Pike*
> *(Army officer, 1809–91)*

most powerful people in the country: business leaders at the Empire Club and Canada's prime minister. She seemed to be just as comfortable with these people as she was with the homeless, for Hannah saw all of them as just people.

Helped by her parents, Hannah's passion became a charitable organization, The Ladybug Foundation. Through donations, fundraising initiatives (including many speaking engagements), the Ladybug Jars, and the sale of items such as scarves bearing the foundation's logo, Hannah has raised more than $2 million for homeless projects across Canada.

She is also very excited to have created a second charitable organization called the Ladybug Foundation Education

Program Inc., whose purpose is to develop Make Change, an education resource for kids across Canada that will empower them to make change in their communities, their country, and their world. Hannah wants every child to have the chances she has had to effect change.

The Ladybug Foundation's website (www.ladybug-foundation.ca) provides suggestions for how kids anywhere can become involved in continuing Hannah's dream. But just as important is the vision behind that dream. Hannah's vision involves hope and recognizes that all people deserve not only a place to live and proper food to eat, but also love, respect, and caring.

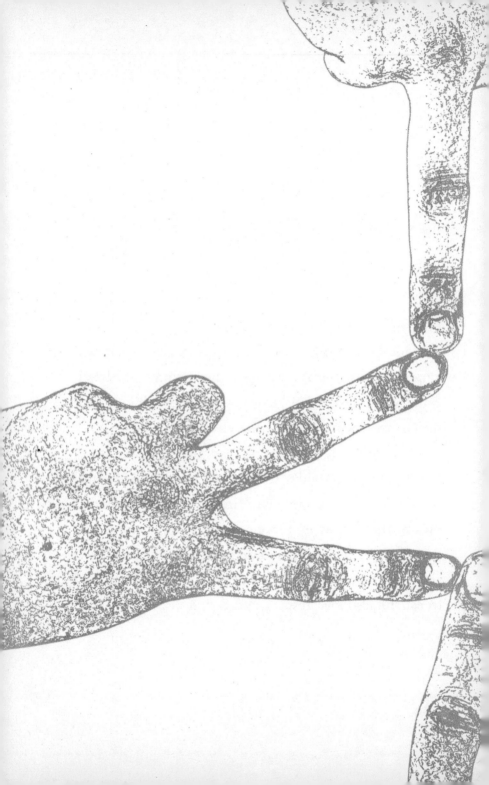

# KYLE

# ANGELOW

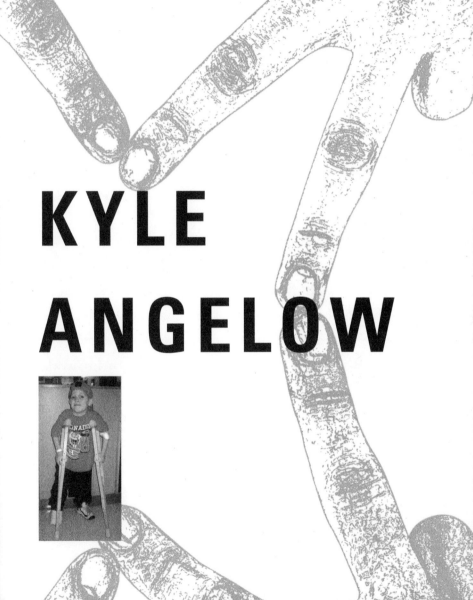

# PICKING UP THE TORCH

Kyle was five and a half years old when the diagnosis was made: Ewing's sarcoma, a type of bone cancer, in his right femur, the largest and strongest bone in the human body, the one that stretches from the knee to the pelvis. Too young to understand what that really meant, Kyle soon learned that it would turn his world upside down and create pain and suffering.

The first step was to give Kyle a type of medication—chemotherapy—to fight the cancer. Because cancer is a strong illness, the medication has to be equally strong. It fights the cancer, working to reduce the size of the tumour—the place where the cancer is growing—and to stop it from spreading to other parts of the body. Kyle was given a port, an opening that leads to one of the major blood vessels travelling directly to his heart. The chemotherapy was dripped intravenously into his bloodstream, sent to do battle with the cancer. It was given to him for different lengths of time. Sometimes he'd receive the medicine continuously for six days, then have three weeks' rest, then have three more days of chemotherapy. This went on for thirteen months.

While the chemotherapy is administered to kill the cancer, it doesn't affect just the cancer cells. It can also cause difficulties with other cells, including killing healthy white cells, which fight against infection and repair damage in the body. In Kyle's case, his white blood cells were significantly weakened and reduced in number. As well, he suffered from side effects of the medication. He couldn't hold down food and was constantly nauseous. Because of this, he lost a great deal of weight and didn't have much energy. Finally, the chemotherapy caused him to lose all of his hair.

The doctors also had to perform surgery on Kyle. The tumour had to be removed. This is where a delicate balancing act occurred. The chemotherapy was necessary to prevent the cancer from spreading but, in reducing the number of his white blood cells, it made him weak and

> That light we see is burning in my hall. /
> How far that little candle throws his beams! / So shines
> a good deed in a naughty world.

*William Shakespeare, from* The Merchant of Venice
*(English playwright, 1564–1616)*

therefore surgery became more risky. A whole team of doctors worked with Kyle and his family to decide when chemotherapy would end and how much time would be necessary for him to regain enough strength to allow the surgery to take place.

The first surgery involved two steps. His right femur, the source of the cancer, was removed. But something needed to take the place of this bone. The lower leg has two bones that stretch from the knee to the ankle. The smaller of these is called the fibula. They removed the fibula from Kyle's *left* leg and placed it where the right femur had been. The surgery was successful, but ultimately the fibula

> Young people are in a unique position to change the world. All we have to do is believe that we can make a difference, and we will.

**Craig Kielburger**
*(Canadian social activist, 1982–)*

cracked and had to be removed. In a thirteen-hour surgery, they replaced it with the fibula from his *right* leg.

At the same time, routine X-rays had identified some spots on Kyle's lungs that could be cancer. He was opened up, his ribs were separated, and these spots were examined. Fortunately, they were not cancerous. In total, Kyle had ten surgeries stretching over a period of almost two years.

During this whole time, his parents were there to help Kyle, all the while feeling his hurt and pain, wishing that it wasn't real, and willing to give up their own lives for the life of their son. Kyle's mother, Kathy, remembers it being like a game of snakes and ladders. Every time they moved forward a step or a level, climbed a ladder, made progress, another bad thing would come up.

Throughout the process, Kyle remained brave, determined, and mentally strong, even when his body was weak. He says that he always knew he'd make it, that he knew he'd get by, that this cancer wasn't going to beat him.

During his treatment, Kyle learned about another young man named Terry Fox. Terry, eighteen and in university, had been diagnosed with a similar form of bone cancer. Terry's right leg was amputated and he went through chemotherapy. Terry wanted to fulfill a dream: to try to run across Canada to raise awareness and funds for

> You cannot live a perfect day without doing something for someone who will never be able to repay you.

**John Wooden**
*(American basketball coach, 1910–)*

cancer research. On one leg, this brave young man ran 42 kilometres a day for 143 days. Ultimately, the cancer that had been in his leg spread to his lungs and he was forced to abandon his run to seek further treatment. Ten months later, the cancer ended his life. But Terry's determination to fight this cancer and his family's efforts to continue his fight through the Terry Fox Foundation has resulted in more than $400 million being raised for cancer research and treatment. At the time Terry was diagnosed, eight out of ten people who got bone cancer died, and all of them lost a leg. Now, because of research, eight out of ten people live and most of them get to keep both of their legs.

Kyle knew that Terry wasn't just an inspiration, but a man whose vision and dream were in part responsible for Kyle keeping his leg and his life. Kyle knew that he owed much to Terry and to the millions of people who had donated money. He also knew that it wasn't enough to simply say thank you, that he needed to carry on Terry's dream to find a cure for cancer.

Kyle decided he wanted to speak out, to tell people not only about what had happened to him, but also that, because of their donations, research was winning the war against cancer, but that that war was far from over. One of Kyle's first speeches was made to five hundred children, but a far larger audience was watching. The speech, along with those by politicians, school officials, and Terry's brother, Darrell Fox, was being broadcast to more than two hundred schools across the Region of Peel. This ceremony was launching a massive effort in which every school in the Region of Peel would host a Terry Fox Run and raise funds for cancer research.

Kyle sat on stage while all of the adults gave their speeches. When it was his turn, he walked up to the microphone, which needed to be. lowered. Kyle's speech, short and passionate, explained what had happened to him, the progress that had been made in treating and curing cancer,

> The influence of a beautiful, helpful, hopeful character is contagious and may revolutionize a whole town.

*Eleanor H. Porter*
*(American writer, 1856–1919)*

and the work that still needed to be done. Everyone present and watching heard his words. The schools in the Region of Peel went on to raise an incredible $1.1 million.

The Peel school campaign was a pilot project for what was hoped to be a national celebration the following year, the twenty-fifth anniversary of Terry Fox's Marathon of Hope. Kyle was once again a spokesperson, meeting with school trustees from across Ontario, trying to convince them that every school should participate. His words were so powerful that they unanimously endorsed the initiative, and the following year more than four thousand schools—up from two thousand the previous year—participated in the National Run Day. In total, more than 10,300 schools across Canada, and more than 3.5 million students, participated in a simultaneous one-day event. The total amount raised was more than double that of the previous year. More than $40 million was donated to the Terry Fox Foundation to continue his legacy of finding a cure for cancer.

Thousands of people, staff and volunteers of the Terry Fox Foundation and people in the community, contributed to this enormous effort to raise awareness and funds. It is difficult to assign responsibility to any one individual, but those who were present when Kyle spoke

> I am only one, but still I am one. I cannot do everything, but still I can do something; and because I cannot do everything, I will not refuse to do something I can do.
>
> *Edward Everett Hale*
> *(American clergyman and author, 1822–1909*

know that his role was pivotal, that this one young man had made a tremendous impact. Kyle had moved from cancer victim, to cancer survivor, to a champion in the fight against cancer.

Terry Fox said, more than twenty-five years ago, that if he couldn't continue, others had to take up the cause. Kyle continues to speak out, giving speeches at community events, and to raise awareness and funds to continue Terry's legacy. Terry died more than a decade before Kyle was born. He didn't know Kyle, but if he had, he would have been proud of him—as we all should be.

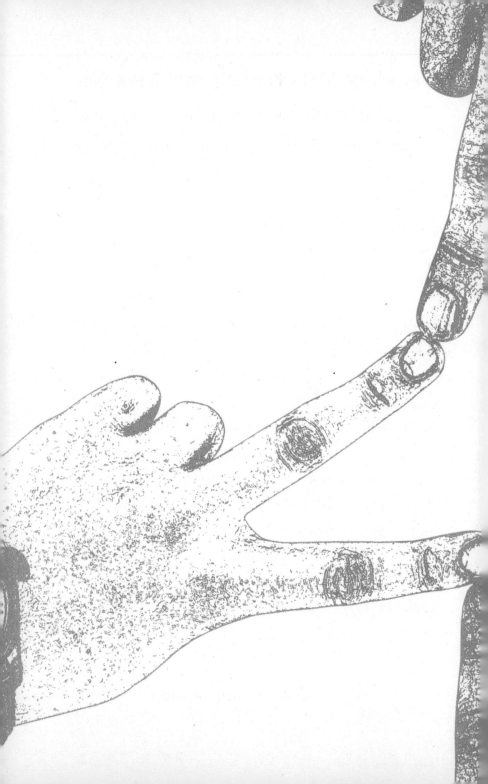

# PAIGE

# PEDLAR

# A STORY ABOUT A STORY

**P**aige Pedlar, like most six-year-old girls, liked to play soccer, swim, skate, spend time with her friends and family, and watch TV. One Sunday morning she and her mother, Anna, were sitting together flipping through the channels. Rather than stopping on Paige's favourite show, *SpongeBob SquarePants,* they started to watch a program about children in Africa who had been orphaned by the death of their parents due to AIDS. Paige sat with her mother and stared at the images that she saw—a life so different than the one she lived with her family. The show ended, but Paige's need to try to understand, to try to make sense of what she'd seen, did not.

Paige's home is filled with pens and paper, crayons and paints. Armed with these supplies, Paige began to write a book. She created from the perspective of a six-year-old, with all the innocence and wisdom that that implies. The first page of her book read:

*Adults, kids and even*
*babies sometimes live*
*alone in Africa because*
*of AIDS. If we all try,*
*we can help them.*
*They really, really, really,*
*need our help!!*

That night, still thinking about what she had seen—small children with no parents to care for them—Paige asked her mother if they could cuddle in bed for a while. Lying there safe and cared for, she thought about those African children and asked, "Who will cuddle the orphans in Africa when they have nightmares?" The next morning, she finished her book.

Creating this book, both words and pictures, helped to clarify things for Paige, helped her to understand—but understanding wasn't enough. As Paige wrote in those first few lines, "If we all try, we can help them." Paige decided that she needed to do more than just write a book; she

You cannot hope to build a better world without improving the individuals. To that end each of us must work for his own improvement, and at the same time share a general responsibility for all humanity, our particular duty being to aid those to whom we think we can be most useful.

*Marie Curie*
*(Polish scientist and two-time Nobel Prize winner, 1867–1935)*

needed to help those children. She decided to make copies of her book and go door to door, selling them to her neighbours. The money she raised would be sent to Africa to help the orphans.

Paige's book soon became known to Joanne Ashley, a member of the Whitby, Ontario, branch of Rotary International, a service organization with millions of members in more than two hundred countries around the world. Paige's story, the support of her family, and the expertise and contacts of Rotary International all led to the publication of her book, *Who Will Cuddle Them When They Sleep?* It has sold approximately 3,000 copies and

Man can now fly in the air like a bird, swim under the ocean like a fish, he can burrow into the ground like a mole. Now if only he could walk the earth like a man, this would be paradise.

**Tommy Douglas**
*(Canadian politician and clergyman, 1904–1986)*

more than $12,000 has been distributed to a variety of organizations since it was created. This money has been used to support the education of AIDS orphans in South Africa, a medical program in Zimbabwe that stops the transmission of the HIV virus from mother to child at birth, and an in-school lunch program for AIDS orphans in Tanzania.

Sitting in her living room, in that same spot where she conceived her book, Paige is able to read letters from the children she has helped. How does that feel? Paige says "It feels great to help people who can't help themselves."

Paige's book has made a difference in the lives of children halfway across the world. Paige is now eleven and in grade six. She's special in the way that all kids are special, but what sets her apart is that she didn't change the channel, she didn't just watch and forget. She decided she wanted to make a difference . . . and she did.

For more information about Paige, how to purchase her book, and her project please visit her website at www.cuddletheorphans.org or e-mail her at www.cuddletheorphans.org.

For more information about Rotary and their projects around the world visit their website at www.rotary.org.

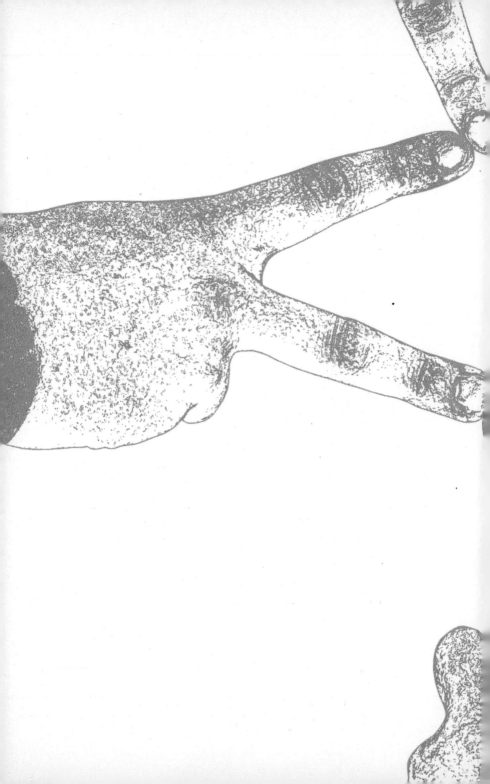

# RYAN HRELJAC

# IT TAKES A FAMILY

Teachers say things to their students that influence them all the time. Usually, they don't know which words affect which students in which ways. But, sometimes they do.

Mrs. Prest talked to her grade one students about how many people in the world do not have access to clean or safe water. Her words were heard by all of her students, but felt most intensely by one of them, six-year-old Ryan Hreljac. Later that day, Ryan measured the distance between his classroom and the drinking fountain in the hall. Nine paces. Certainly much less than the kilometres that separated many children from safe water. Ryan decided, right then, that he had to try to help those children. His goal was to earn $70—enough, he thought, to build a well.

Doing extra chores around the house, Ryan worked to raise the funds. It was a lot of money, but not unreachable. And besides, those kids without water needed his help. It took weeks for Ryan to finally reach his goal. He then discovered that the amount necessary for a well wasn't $70 but *$2000*. He figured that if he could raise the first amount, he could raise the second—it would just take more time. It took time, but Ryan accomplished his goal. That was, of course, just the beginning.

Today, more than eleven years later, the Ryan's Well Foundation has built 461 wells in 16 countries that provide clean and safe water to almost 600,000 people. It started with one six-year-old boy, but it took a whole family, supported by people in the community, to turn the dreams and vision of one young person into this amazing reality.

Ryan's parents, Mark and Susan, supported Ryan's efforts, in the same way they support the efforts and interests of their other children, Jordan and Keegan. By helping Ryan to raise that first amount—$2000—they supported him in his quest. That first well was dug at Angolo

> ## Tenderness and kindness are not signs of weakness and despair, but manifestations of strength and resolution.
>
> **Kahlil Gibran**
> *(Lebanese philosopher, 1883–1931)*

Primary School, near the village of Agweo in northern Uganda.

At the next step, trying to raise $25,000 to purchase a drilling rig, Ryan's parents became more hesitant. Mark, a police detective, and Susan, a government consultant, obviously understood the enormous task that Ryan was undertaking, one that Ryan's tender age safeguarded him from fully comprehending.

Parents always want to ensure the well-being of their children. Perhaps it becomes even more important when your full-time job is being a police officer and you get to see the problems and dangers of the world. Mark

I expect to pass through this world but once. Any good, therefore, that I can do or any kindness I can show to any fellow creature, let me do it now. Let me not defer or neglect it for I shall not pass this way again.

*Stephen Grellet*
*(French religious leader, 1773–1855)*

needed to make sure his son wouldn't be hurt or disappointed, that he wasn't being set up for failure, and that his efforts wouldn't negatively affect the family.

With the help of some supportive people in their community, Ryan's parents decided that Ryan's ongoing work would be facilitated through the creation of an organization—a foundation. The Ryan's Well Foundation began in a spare room of the family home. The phone rang at all hours of the day and night as people around the world called the foundation, not realizing that they weren't calling just a business or an answering machine but Ryan and his family. More than one caller was shocked to find themselves talking to Ryan himself, or his mother, father, or one of his brothers.

From the very beginning, the whole family was involved in the foundation. Ryan's older brother, Jordan, took responsibility for editing and writing the newsletter, answering the phone, doing all of the audiovisual set-up, and making presentations himself. All of this while maintaining his own volunteer interests around social justice and environmental issues, and coaching and refereeing basketball. Keegan, only three when all of this began, started out licking stamps, and has now become the foundation's official photographer while travelling and

It's the action, not the fruit of the action, that's important. You have to do the right thing. It may not be in your power, may not be in your time, that there'll be any fruit. But that doesn't mean you stop doing the right thing. You may never know what results come from your action. But if you do nothing, there will be no results.

**Mahatma Gandhi**
*(Indian politician, activist, and visionary, 1869–1948)*

connecting with people at presentations. Both parents have travelled with Ryan as he has made presentations around the world. Mark uses part of his holidays every year to travel to Africa so he can personally inspect projects the foundation has undertaken there, often in areas that are potentially dangerous.

Susan has taken on the day-to-day responsibility of running the foundation. While also working full-time, she has invested an average of thirty to forty hours per week in the foundation. On two occasions she took a leave of absence from her job to devote even more time to helping the foundation evolve and thrive. Along with the very important tasks of answering phones, writing letters, and organizing, she has travelled extensively with Ryan to present at conferences around the world.

During a visit to the first well created by the foundation, Ryan met Jimmy, one of the boys in the village, and someone Ryan had been pen pals with for over a year. Their friendship continued after Ryan and his family returned to Canada as they continued their correspondence. Jimmy's situation in Uganda was desperate: he was separated from his parents and siblings, living with an aunt and uncle, and his entire part of Uganda was stricken with poverty and in the midst of a civil war.

Because of these terrible things, Ryan's family decided that Jimmy's future was not in Uganda but with them.

For the past five-and-a-half years, Jimmy has lived with Ryan and his family. He has become the fourth son, the fourth brother. Jimmy has become not only a member of the family but also an active participant in the foundation. From speaking engagements, to helping with day-to-day tasks, to inspiring others with his energy, enthusiasm, and engaging smile, he is helping to bring about the foundation's goals.

As the foundation grew and its work became better known, more and more demands were placed on Ryan

> Adhere to truth, for truth leads to good deeds and good deeds leads him who does them to paradise.

**Muhammad**
*(Prophet and founder of Islam, 570–632)*

and his siblings. Mark and Susan made sure that these demands wouldn't take away from the normal activities of childhood. Speaking engagements, including international television appearances, were postponed or scheduled to allow the boys to participate in sporting events, attend family functions, or just be kids. The guidance and direction of Ryan's parents have ensured that this remains, first and foremost, a family.

While it takes a family to form and create a foundation, the very heart of the Ryan's Well Foundation is Ryan himself. Since the beginning, it has been Ryan's vision, passion, and simple refusal to accept limitations

**Do all the good you can, by all the means you can, in all the ways you can, in all the places you can, at all the times you can, to all the people you can, as long as ever you can.**

*John Wesley*
*(English clergy and Methodist founder, 1703–1778)*

that has driven the foundation. He has travelled to 32 countries, made more than 350 presentations, and spoken to more than 600,000 people. He has worked to educate people, raise funds and awareness, and inspire others to do their part.

His message is simple: "Be kind. Be compassionate. Care and share what you have with others. Get involved in your communities and get involved in the world."

# ACKNOWLEDGEMENTS

I would like to extend my deepest thanks to the administrative assistants, personal assistants, secretaries, partners, and parents who help guide the creative forces of the people who contributed to this book. I think we all know that without you, this book, and *so* much more, would never be accomplished.

A special thanks to my editor, Amy Black, for believing.

# ABOUT THE AUTHOR

**Eric Walters**, trained as a teacher, social worker and family therapist, has often written about issues that are troubling and contentious. Through his work and writing, he has strived to help young people to understand real-world issues and their possible solutions. He donated all of his royalties from his book *Run* to the Terry Fox Foundation and the idea for the National Run Day of the Foundation was conceived at his dining room table. He helped to run the pilot project that convinced the Fox family and foundation of the merit of this idea. In the end, over 10,000 schools across the country participated in a one-day event to continue Terry's fight to raise funds to cure cancer. Other books have helped to fund children's programs in Uganda (*When Elephants Fight*) provided funds to an orphanage in Rwanda (*Shattered*), and Eric presently runs an outreach program in Kenya, The Creation of Hope, which provides opportunity and hope to children in Kikima, Kenya.

Eric Walters speaks to over 100,000 young people every year, talking to them not just about literacy, but about how they can make a difference in the world. He believes very strongly that it is important for people not to merely *tell* what they believe, but to *show* what they believe.